MW00629994

Money
in Your Hands

Kay Packard
Guadalajara Jal.
July 14, 2023

Money
In Your Hands

*Use the Map Hidden in Your Hands
to Navigate Your Path to
Financial Freedom*

Kay Packard

2021 · Pioneer Press
Three Rivers, California

Copyright © 2021 by Kay Packard

All rights reserved

Printed in the United States of America

ISBN 978-0-9907179-1-1

Pioneer Press

Post Office Box 321

Three Rivers, California 93271

Contents

Gift Markings
Flagships for Financial Fulfillment 118

Preface

IMPRINTED IN YOUR OWN TWO HANDS is a map to help you uncover hidden riches of wealth, wisdom and prosperity. Yes, your personalized money map is inscribed into the palms of your hands like a treasure map. If you're ready to make more money, you can!

With a little information and my guidance, you can learn to decode these messages about yourself and use them to create your most amazing money experience. What I teach you will assist you in weaving together both the understood and misunderstood aspects of yourself so that you can take steps to manifest the cornucopia you want while finding fulfillment living your best life.

The contents of this book are based on my eighteen years of hand reading experience and more than 200 hours of content-rich material I have developed, practiced and taught to students around the world since 2005. One reason I'm assembling it now is because an editor from a prestigious magazine recently asked me to write about the "money line" in the hand. She asked because the 7.6 million magazine readership, of which 90% are women, want insights into generating more money so they can worry less about their families and their future. Another more important reason is that I firmly believe that women, mothers and young adults better equipped with money-making intelligence, strategies and mindsets will make for an incredibly better world. Everyone has specialized talents that are unmistakably identifiable in their own two hands.

My objective is to offer you guidance to relate more deeply, confidently and powerfully with your inner resources. You have extraordinary potential that is calling to come through you. Why would everyone have unique designs imprinted in their hands unless they were meant to be read? I'm not asking you to take my word for it; I'm asking you to try it for yourself, and see how it works for you. See for yourself how your life can be positively transformed. Put this content to test. You can always go back to your old ways of thinking and acting when it comes to the almighty dollar.

Do you want financial freedom? Can you imagine boundless fortunes? Napoleon Hill said, "If you do not see great riches in your imagination, you will never see them in your bank balance." Let's combine your desires and your imagination with your own two hands and the personalized treasure map encoded there!

All cultures, nationalities and gender identities are honored and accepted here. I prioritize human dignity and deeply honor the life *you* are designing. Current grammar rules have been followed while editing this book. Referencing he, she, him, and her is not intended to restrict any reader's preference of expression. Adapt the terms noted the way you want so that you make the most of the contents.

Money
in Your Hands

Introduction

"Perseverance pays off."
—*Charles R. Schwab*

IF YOU HAVE EVER wondered about a hidden money map being encoded into your hands, or if you're just discovering this idea and want to learn more, this book is for you. *Money in Your Hands* is about you mining the treasures buried in your hands and shaping and manifesting your money story, applying the wisdom revealed in the inscriptions in your own hands. It's time to take control of your money story getting from where you are to where you want to be.

I hope to inspire you to reveal the secret symbols in your own hands so you can:

+ Observe and rearrange your mental money habits

+ Transcend limitations by revealing unconscious money patterns

+ Remove obstacles to creating more wealth

+ Open your mind to unlimited possibilities

+ Know and use your natural talents at remarkable levels

+ Tune into and align with your higher wisdom

+ Understand your personal motives

+ See with fresh perspective

+ Consciously make new life choices

+ Clearly recognize and fully embrace your strengths

+ Shine light on your weaknesses and use them as allies in hiding

+ Get clear on the money breakthroughs you want in your life and create powerful strategies to achieve them

At this basic level of hand analysis, I focus on a non-predictive and accurate approach to decoding the natural line formations, hand and finger shapes, and unique fingerprint patterns. There are postive and negative possibilities to each identifiable attribute in the hands. Each characteristic of the hand, be it the Heart Line, Gift Marking, hand shape, Challenge Marking, Wisdom Marking or Fate Line, has both positive and negative connotations. The key is to leverage both as we do with the sunlight during the day and the stars and moonlight by night.

I would like to make one thing clear before going any further: I'm not offering a method of fortune-telling, psychic reading, or predictive techniques. I am not a financial consultant. This is about you discovering and listening to your inner wisdom related to the language coded in your hands in now-time. Your hands have very specific etchings that are the result of the neurological byways and highways that race through your brain waves and psyche. The topography of the skin on your palms and fingers can be decoded to reveal your special talents, attributes, preferences and strengths, as well as your weaknesses and challenges. Attractions, distractions and irritations in your emotional, physical, mental and spiritual realms can be identified and interpreted. Ideal career, business and relationship scenarios can also be revealed.

Be aware also that the lines in your hands are not permanent, but can change. That's right—they can change. Markings appear and disappear with time. The system you'll be learning focuses on what is present at the time you look at the hands. Each marking has a positive and a negative interpretation. The positive interpretation describes your innate personal power operating at its fullest potential. The negative interpretation relates to a trait that is either under- or overused. With awareness you can capitalize on the feature as an ally in disguise.

All negative possibilities offer shadow wisdom. Shadows are created by light. We grow stronger as we open to our pitfalls and shine the light of awareness on them. You'll learn to use your drawbacks, bring them to the light and bloom into your highest and best life.

We generally move through the day unconsciously. Now is the time to be more conscious of your talents and skills so that you can aim them, like an arrow to the bullseye, to gain financial independence. Your success depends on you. Isn't it time to take charge?

How to Use This Book

1. Read through, page by page, and identify markings in your hands with correlating illustrations found in this book.

2. At the same time, record the markings you see in the blank hand maps at the back of the book in the Appendix.

3. Read and contemplate deeply the strengths, pitfalls, money mind-sets, breakthrough questions and affirmations associated with those described.

4. Take the short amount of time suggested to complete the exercise at the end of each chapter. These exercises are designed to assist you in integrating the positive and negative explanations of these markings.

5. Transfer selected markings into your personalized Manifest My Money Map and Plan for Financial Freedom exercises in the Appendix at the back of the book. Here, you'll be guided to integrate an assortment of markings to get a more precise picture to help create the financial future you want.

I suggest you look at the exercise at the end of each chapter before you start reading the chapter so you get a feel for what you'll be filling in. You're also encouraged to look at the exercises in the Appendix before starting so you'll know what you'll be filling in there too. You are welcome to photo-copy these templates from the book or visit MoneyInYourHandsBook.com to download and print.

Derived directly from the markings, your use of these tips, mindset declarations and your answers to the breakthrough questions will raise you into realizing your highest money potential. If you don't, who will? Besides answering the questions in the book, you may want to record your findings and key take-aways in a designated companion journal, on index cards, video recordings or voice memos. You might enjoy having a study buddy to read through the materials and learn together. Whatever way works best for your learning and advancement, it's time to step into your genius zone.

Because I'm a fan of Florence Scovel Shinn, who wrote many books on become successful using the universal laws that govern life, I include affirmations she created where I considered appropriate with some markings. Use the affirmations when it feels right and is convincing to you. Modify them slightly if that better serves you. In *The Secret Door to Success*, Shinn wrote, "You must have a great desire for financial freedom, you must feel yourself rich, you must see yourself rich, you must continually prepare for riches. Become as a little child and make believe you are rich. You are then impressing the subconscious with expectancy. The imagination is man's workshop, the scissors of the mind, where he is constantly cutting out the events of his life!"

Within this book, expect to find precise and reliable information for interpreting the secret money code in your hands. At minimum, try an experiment: recite the strengths, money mindsets and affirmations with conviction and feeling. For extra credit, besides completing the exercises in the book, keep a notebook to accompany your reading so that you have plenty of space to record your newfound awareness as you unearth your inherent treasures. In essence, you are in charge of defining your destiny. This book will show you how.

What's My Highest Money Potential?

Many people who have shown me their hands have asked, "Will I make money?" A better question to ask is, "What is the best way for *me* to make money?" I ask you, "What is it about money that you want most?" My job is to help you discover your highest money potential and increase your fortune. You are a unique, one-of-a-kind person who has special talents, remarkable dreams, personalized goals, an individualized level of vitality and a certain emotional drive that needs to be ascertained so that you're most effective in creating your riches. This is where your hands come in handy (no pun intended).

Speaking of rich, here's one of my favorite definitions of rich: Able to afford all the things and experiences required to fully experience your most authentic life. (Jen Sincero, *You're a Badass at Making Money*). What does an authentic life mean for you?

I especially love Jen's definition because the crux of the meaning is you living your authentic life and to me that means you're in full alignment with who you are; you're living in integrity, congruent with your gifts, dreams, values and your inner wisdom. Unlimited resources are available while operating as your true self because you have access to higher realms of possibility and imagination.

For you to feel true prosperity you must become a metaphorical sculptor of your life by simply removing from your life everything that isn't the sculpture. As an example, this includes inherited thoughts, beliefs you assumed to be true and prescribed actions dictated to you. Take time to look and see for yourself what has been told to you over and over by your parents, teachers, peers and society. Some long-term stories may no longer serve you. Without becoming the sculptor of your own money story, others' stories will continue to govern your precious life, including your pocketbook.

While an advice-giver is usually well intended when influencing you in a direction toward financial reward, the counsel is coming from that person's life-perspective. That person's hurdles are not your hurdles. His or her strengths, motives and drive are most likely not the same as yours. Sure, take the best and leave the rest *and* get clear about your optimum path to cash.

Imagine someone having narrow hands with smooth skin and long and skinny fingers. Would an advice-giver who has a very successful auto shop be successful telling this narrow-handed person that he or she would do well to work on cars as a mechanic? Intuitively, you may gather that mechanics have wider, squarish palms with rougher skin and shorter fingers (for holding tools), not narrow, soft-skinned hands with long, skinny fingers. Square-handed people are practical and productive. Narrow-handed people are sensitive and nurturing. Before taking risks, carefully consider the source of the advice being given.

My first question is "Do you want money?" and if so, "Why?" The first of many exercises I'll be giving you in this book is to, now, use the designated area below or get a sheet of paper. At the top of the workspace write a number representing the gross amount of money you want to receive in the next six months. Then list all the reasons why you want that money. Choose a three-month window if it's easier. Or if you prefer, go for a twelve-month timespan. The key is to search out your requirements and desires for money, along with a specific amount within a defined time frame.

In the next six months I want to receive $_____.

What I will do with the money:

_____

_____

_____

Think about what you want to experience and what you will do with the money created.

I want this money because (be specific):

_____

_____

_____

What was your experience with writing an amount of money you want to receive in the next six months? Did the number come easily? Did you stumble? Did you get specific with your reasons for wanting the money? Or were you vague about your purposes for wanting the money?

If you stumbled, take more time to complete this exercise. Go deep. You're diving into and beyond the subconscious mind where your mental money habits are stored under lock and key. These habits are often times inherited from family, friends and society. If you're really tripped up, we need to find and dismantle your blocks to creating more wealth. Working with this book will engage your aversions to money.

To help unveil your highest money potential and illuminate what it is about money you most want, here's one exercise I found more profound than any other: Hand write a letter to Money. Start your letter with:

Dear Money,

_____

_____

_____

_____

Keep this letter to Money. After reading about the markings in your hands and doing the exercises, look for correlations between what you learned and your mindsets. In six months write another letter to Money. Notice where your outlook may have shifted. I highly recommend you do write this letter so that you become aware of your true relationship with money.

To help you answer the question, "What is the best way for *me* to make money?" you'll decode the glyphs in your own two hands while dissecting your true desires and adjusting your mindsets. Use the symbols stamped in your hands as a blueprint for declaring your worth, capitalizing on your strengths and shoring up your weaknesses so that you can, strategize, create, attract and manifest more money in your life, starting now.

Playing It Safe

Oftentimes, people get into fields of work where they believe they'll be safe and make the amount of money that is pre-set in their mind. External influences are absorbed into the subconscious mind at various times in life and the result is a mindset with a glass ceiling.

To generate revenue, it's crucial to uncover your internal blocks to a plentiful flow of money. Certain markings in the hands will pinpoint the themes of your personal money obstacles. You'll do best to use those hurdles as road signs to decide on new directions to aim your mental patterns and precious energy so that you can break that glass money ceiling and make more money.

Limiting mindsets I've heard:

"Mom or dad made xx amount of money, so that is about as good as I'll be able to do."

"I have children to raise and put through school, so I have to keep doing this job (that I hate)."

"It takes money to make money, and I don't have what I need!"

"If I make more money, I'll appear greedy."

"I feel guilty making this amount of money."

"I need to make money to survive."

"Someone, like the bank, the government, the IRS or a hacker will get to my money if I don't spend it or hide it under my mattress."

"If I make more money certain people in my family will ask me for it, and I don't know how to say no."

"If I make more money my male mate will feel emasculated."

"My partner wants to be the primary breadwinner and wants me to stay home with the kids."

"If I want more money, I'll have to work harder."

"If I follow my passion and quit this job, I don't believe I can make as much money as I'm making now."

"If I increase the fees for my services, I'll lose longtime clients."

"It's not spiritual to charge a fee and make money."

After reading the above statements, what comes up for you?

What beliefs are holding you back from receiving more money?

In the book *Solving Yourself*, Wu Hsin said, "Beliefs are the string on which all misunderstandings are strung. As an animal tied to a post wanders only within the length of its rope, one can only go as far as one's beliefs allow." To manage and change your beliefs, you must pinpoint and question them. The mind is a good servant but not a good master. In short, your thoughts about money are more important than the amount you have. Let's create a bankroll breakthrough with a revised money story where you are the master.

Your Money Map <u>Is</u> in Your Hands

"You have brains in your head. You have feet in your shoes. You can steer yourself any direction you choose."
—Dr. Seuss

TO DECIPHER YOUR money map, we'll start with the basics in the hand. Within your mighty hands are many features to explore. The shape, fingers, lines and markings in the hand can be interpreted to define particular components of your personality and psychology. What you like and dislike can be deciphered from what is inscribed in your hands. Blending a combination of three or more markings together will illustrate how you are different from everyone else. I'd like to introduce you to some fundamentals of hand analysis here. It's simple to get started. Depending on your desire and motivation, advanced levels can also be mastered. But in this book, we'll keep it simple and focus primarily on illuminating fortunes precisely scribed in the natural line formations on your palms and characteristics of your fingers and thumbs.

The basic hand map (Figure 1) shows the primary landscape of the hand. The high-level descriptions of the thumb, fingers and mounts come from the ancient art and science of hand reading. You will be introduced to an expanded yet simple vocabulary as you read through this book. The major lines are also identified in Figure 1.

This guidebook will help you analyze the following features and carvings in your hands in particular association with producing wealth while advancing you on your path to financial freedom.

- ✦ Fate Lines
- ✦ Challenge Markings
- ✦ Head Lines types
- ✦ Fingers, finger sections and finger spacing
- ✦ Gift and Wisdom Markings
- ✦ The thumb
- ✦ Basic hand shapes
- ✦ Heart Lines

No one marking in either the right or the left hand will reveal your entire money map. In fact, one pattern in the hand may contradict another in the same or other hand. For example, someone with a Late Bloomer (Figure 7) indicator on one hand may have the Determined

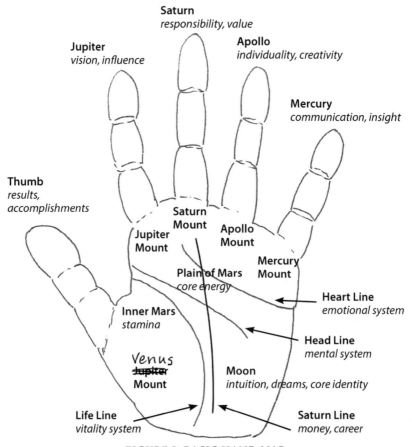

FIGURE I: BASIC HAND MAP

configuration (Figure 10) in the other. In this, and all cases, both variables must be evaluated together to point the owner to the highest possible potential. A variety of areas in the topography of your hands must be examined, specifically the features listed above. Blending various symbols together pinpoints capabilities and specific tactics to implement for creating more money. Markings in the hands will also indicate potential loss of fortune, and how.

The Fate Line has traditionally been aligned with money so we'll look their first.

The Fate Line

Your Destiny Depends on the Direction of Your Aim

> *"You are the master of your destiny."*
> *—Napoleon Hill*

THE TRADITIONALLY known Fate Line is a vertical line rising from the base of the palm toward the middle finger and is more appropriately called the Line of Saturn (Figure 2). It's also been called the Career Line, the Line of Destiny, and the Money Line. Saturn energy urges one to accomplish tasks through extended work and responsibility *over time.*

The length, quality and quantity of lines under the middle finger are interpreted to understand how the owner demonstrates responsibility through effort and direction with worldly affairs. Effort is made through organization, structure and discipline. Experience and knowledge support organizational skills. We typically see these Saturnian characteristics in work, projects and careers. As organized effort and commitment is put forth in a systematic method over time, money predictably appears. This sounds serious, but it can be fun, too. Engage your whole heart and reap results more rapidly.

Reward follows as we progress with integrity. Integrity is when your outer and inner worlds are in alignment, where the outer self reflects the inner self. For example, you love nature and plan vacations to national parks to enjoy mountains, trees and wildlife with your family. Integrity could be compromised by investing in oil drilling, which is disruptive to the environment and destroys nature habitats.

All variables and markings involving Saturn call us to balance our

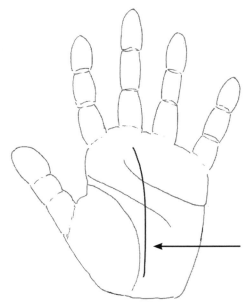

FIGURE 2: SATURN LINE

inner and outer worlds, the active and passive sides of the hand—the thumb side being active and the opposite edge side of the hand being passive. Most hands have a Saturn Line appearing in some form or another. We'll explore many examples. Some hands don't have a Saturn Line. You'll learn what that means, too.

The words Fate and Saturn represent the same line. Using this line in a broad sense, a strength, pitfall, money mindset and breakthrough question have been assigned in the following example.

> STRENGTH: I am effectively aligned with the appropriate task.

> PITFALL: Dedication to tasks at the expense of enjoyment and relationships.

> MONEY MINDSET: I live with joy, as I am balanced in my responsibilities, commitments, integrity and vocation.

> BREAKTHROUGH QUESTION: Is [this] expenditure in alignment with my values?

Saturn energy is involved when we take care of business at the micro and macro levels. The universal lesson of Saturn is self-worth. We labor and accomplish to show worth. We like to see value in return for accomplishment. Saturn creates structure to complete tasks. In the process, the inside is watching the outside; this is integrity. Ideally, our livelihood is congruent with our personal values and integrity. Such is not always the case!

Saturn Line Origination Points

The location on the hand where the Saturn Line starts provides a reliable pointer as to the Saturnian influence one will see in their life. The starting point of the line is usually in the lower half of the palm and rises upward toward the fingers, like a tree grows to the sky.

Money through Family

The owner of a Saturn Line starting inside the Life Line (Figure 3) and rising up the hand, makes money through family business, goals and assets. His or her vocation is influenced by family ties.

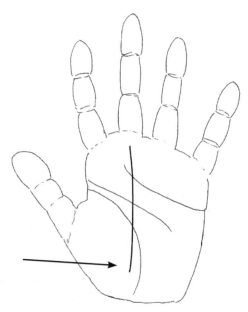

FIGURE 3: MONEY THROUGH FAMILY

I ask my clients with this configuration, "Will you take over the family farm, real estate company or investment firm? Are you reaping the benefits of a long-term family investment? Do your values align with the family?" Family may also include an associated clan for many years such as a religious organization or a membership community.

Sticking with the status quo and resisting change is an obstacle with this marking. Milking cows for business is no longer done by hand. Instead of selling mansions, success in real estate can come through flipping properties for profit.

> STRENGTH: Access to family assets and business is developed and increased over time.

> PITFALL: Stuck in "this is the way it's always been done."

> MONEY MINDSET: I add tremendous value to the family business and I am worthy of generous compensation for my dedication, loyalty and ability to adapt to change.

> BREAKTHROUGH QUESTIONS: Could letting go of "that's the way it's always been done" benefit the business in any way? What fresh perspective could I embrace so that I generate more revenue and create a solid foundation for future generations?

> AFFIRMATION: "I am now deluged with the happiness that was planned for me in the Beginning. My barns are full, my cup flows over with joy." —Florence Scovel Shinn

The Eternal Student

You love learning something new if the Saturn Line starts high on the Life Line in your hand (Figure 4). You enjoy taking classes, getting certificates and degrees into your forties, fifties and beyond.

You are a perfect candidate to become financially free as long as you study and *implement* the laws of money. *Rich Dad, Poor Dad* by Robert Kiyosaki offers financial education content to help readers learn about cash flow, assets, liabilities, real estate, and investing. T. Harv Eker, author of *Secrets of a Millionaire Mind*, presents a collection of mental attitudes that facilitate wealth. His theory is that we each possess a financial blueprint or an internal script that dictates how we relate to money, and that by changing this blueprint people can change their ability to accumulate wealth. Learning about and executing the million-aire mind declarations Eker presents could present massive financial payoff.

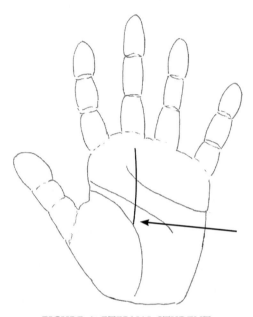

FIGURE 4: ETERNAL STUDENT

Complete this sentence: As a person who balances the costs of tuition and generating revenue, I decide to take action by…

_____

_____

_____

_____

One Eternal Student answered this question with, "committing to for-mulate and execute a plan to make money with what I learn, with my first goal being to earn back the tuition."

STRENGTH: I feel enriched when learning something new, and I have impressive credentials.

PITFALL: Limited income while taking course after course.

MONEY MINDSET: I balance my desire to take new classes with determination to generate revenue through financial intelligence.

BREAKTHROUGH QUESTIONS: What is it about having the certifications that is most important to me? What is in my "well of opportunities" to make money while I sleep using something I've already learned? What's my plan for return-on-investment with my current learning adventure?

AFFIRMATION: "I give thanks that the millions which are mine by Divine Right, now pour in and pile up under grace in perfect ways." —Florence Scovel Shinn

It is possible to have one type of Fate Line on one hand and another type on the other hand. Blending the meaning of both configurations paints a bigger picture for the owner. For example, when combining the last two maps (Money through Family and Eternal Student), the owner would bring benefit to the family business with continual learning. It's also possible to have two types of Fate Lines on one hand. If this is the case, both formations would be interpreted to decipher the nature of commitment.

Intuitively Guided

Do either of your hands have a Saturn Line stretching from the lower outer side of palm, called the Moon Mount (Figure 5) up toward your middle finger?

If so, this is a strong indicator that you always seem to be in the right place at the right time, as long as you're tuned into your instincts. Pay close attention to your hunches. Start a journal to track your inklings related to anything—especially money.

The moon relates to imagination, inner trust, intuition and the

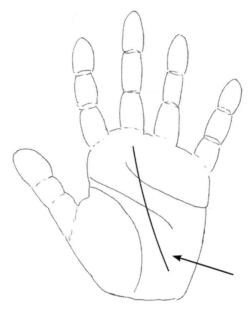

FIGURE 5: INTUITIVELY GUIDED

subconscious. With this marking, you are spiritually (nonmaterial, metaphysical, something greater than yourself) motivated. Give space to your mystical pursuits. Allow space for new ideas and clues to present themselves. Letting go of extreme logic will assist you in making more money. You must believe in what you're doing.

You might find this line on a dream interpreter, animal whisperer, storyteller, dancer or a public relations specialist.

> STRENGTH: My intuition is sharp and accurate. I never argue with a hunch.
>
> PITFALL: Relying too much on logic and reason.
>
> MONEY MINDSET: I am in the right place at the right time to engage in inspirational and meaningful work both to give and receive prosperity.
>
> BREAKTHROUGH QUESTIONS: How might my bank account increase if I align with my intuitive self 10% more often? 50% more often? Three occasions I felt

prosperous after following a hunch were... [*List three occasions.*]

AFFIRMATION: "Never do today what intuition says to do tomorrow." —Florence Scovel Shin

Transformation Specialist

When the Saturn Line starts on the outer, middle side of the palm just below the Heart Line and climbs toward the base of the middle finger (Figure 6), the owner will find treasures in a career or line of work changing lives, guiding people through radical change and rebirth. It's natural for this person to be comfortable with grief associated with sudden trauma.

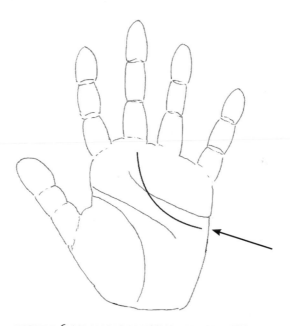

FIGURE 6: TRANSFORMATION SPECIALIST

If you have this marking, you're likely to understand the components of change in a profound way. Being a change manager would be right up your alley. Perhaps you navigate individuals or organizations through expected responses during loss, which include:

+ stability before change
+ immobilization with shock and disbelief
+ denial
+ trying to regain control through anger
+ bargaining
+ depression
+ experimenting through time
+ acceptance

Transformation Specialists work as plastic surgeons, makeup artists, corporate restructure consultants, change managers, demolition engineers, funeral home directors, grief counselors and hospice workers.

Other markings in the hands can also show gifts for guiding people through unexpected twists and turns in life. The Pluto Star is one such marking and will be discussed in a later chapter on Gift Markings.

> STRENGTH: I instinctively understand transformation and use my expertise to effectively guide people through life changes.
>
> PITFALL: Lost in an unhealed loss.
>
> MONEY MINDSET: I am profitable helping people, groups and organizations navigate change because my finesse, experience and skills are highly valued.
>
> BREAKTHROUGH QUESTIONS: Would letting go of something or someone serve me so I can move forward making more money? How have unexpected changes in my life served my role as a change agent? Who were the last three people who complimented me on my understanding of change and ability to help them through an unexpected and undesirable situation in their lives?
>
> AFFIRMATION: "God works in unexpected places, through unexpected people, at unexpected times, His wonders to perform." —Florence Scovel Shinn

Late Bloomer

When the Saturn Line starts in the middle of palm and climbs upward (Figure 7) you catch on to responsibility, work and commitment later in life. Richard Unger named this configuration the Late Bloomer. This is a strong indicator that you were able to play as a child and remained a free-spirit into your young adult life. At some point your rocket of direction was ignited and you chose a particular direction to excel.

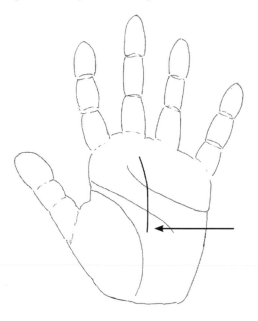

FIGURE 7: LATE BLOOMER

If you own this design and you notice your high-achieving graduating high school friends taking flight for college, trade school, art school or starting to take the band on tour, and you're not, please know there is nothing wrong with you. Enjoy your wandering. One day you'll feel the lightning strike and, on your way, you will fly, as the bird you're meant to be. In the book *Jonathan Livingston Seagull*, Jonathan, the seagull who broke out of conformity, said, "Your only obligation in any lifetime is to be true to yourself."

Rich Karlgaard, author of *Late Bloomers*, addresses what it means to be a Late Bloomer in today's world obsessed with early achievement. In a blog post he says, "What late bloomers need to do is get off the early bloomer conveyor belt and find a new path of discovery." Karlgaard cites a number of Late Bloomers who found their way and are in perfect positions for them, many quite successful in society's view.

While parents may think their young adult is floundering between interests and friends, it could not be more opposite because the Late Bloomer is actually flourishing toward what's to come. I advise parents to be patient and supportive of their offsprings' natural path. There is no need to push the young one onto the early bloomer conveyor belt, which will certainly lead to failure and heartbreak. The day will come for this youth to take bloom on his or her supreme quest.

> STRENGTH: I've observed how people make their way in life and I've enjoyed the pace at which I have pursued my passions and unique talents regardless of societal approval.

> PITFALL: I can't, I'm too far behind, I missed the boat.

> MONEY MINDSET: I am eager to dig in, carve my unique path and build a solid wealth-generating foundation.

> BREAKTHROUGH QUESTIONS: What would have to be true for me to believe in myself as wildly successful in *my* vocation of choice regardless of public approval? What one area of my life do I most want to pursue, and how would it look to follow through according to my definition(s) of completion?

> AFFIRMATION: "Be not weary of make-believing. When you least expect it you shall reap." —Florence Scovel Shinn

Absent Saturn Line

Don't be surprised if one or both hands is missing a Saturn Line entirely. If a hand doesn't have a vertical line rising to the Saturn finger, its owner is more inclined to drift along without a plan. This doesn't mean she won't work hard, but if she does, it will most likely be in a direction that someone else has defined. The good news is that this person has the freedom to shape her own way in the world, at her own pace.

STRENGTH: I'm easygoing at the pace that best suits me.

PITFALL: Directionless, frustrated with outside pressure.

MONEY MINDSET: Carving my path to financial freedom is my choice to make and fulfill.

BREAKTHROUGH QUESTIONS: As a small child, what did I want to do, more than anything else, when I grew up? What's the truest desire of my heart now? How could these dreams be monetized?

AFFIRMATION: "I embrace the rhythm of life and let it unfold." —Fearless Motivation

Family Feedback

When the origination point of the Saturn Line twists around the Life Line at the base of the hand (Figure 8) the owner will usually seek counsel from the family before moving in a particular direction.

Decisions for going to college or starting a business, traveling the

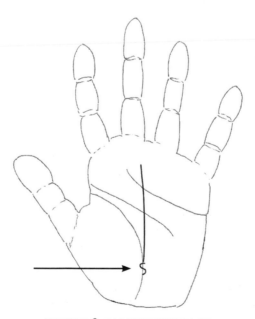

FIGURE 8: FAMILY FEEDBACK

world or starting a family, taking the job offer in Shanghai or New York won't be made without consulting first with trusted members in the family, community or tribe. The Life Line associated with family roots and the Saturn Line of direction are commingled for a short length, therefore the owner seriously contemplates input from the grounded, reliable, consistent nature of "family" before making final decisions.

The upside is having a strong network of people to rely upon. The downside is losing sight of your own passions that are out of sync with the family.

> STRENGTH: I have a solid circle of family and mentors who give me beneficial feedback to remain aligned with my core values.

> PITFALL: Too much reliance on what "they say" and remain stuck.

> MONEY MINDSET: I weigh advice from worthy sources in my tribe and make courageous money decisions.

> BREAKTHROUGH QUESTIONS: Would I lose anything by letting go of an unwarranted opinion or project? If I could do anything I wanted, and would feel most fulfilled in doing so, what would that be? Precisely, how are my roots helping to create the fruits of my fortunes?

> AFFIRMATION: "My happiness is built upon a rock. It is mine now for all eternity." —Florence Scovel Shinn

Busy, Busy

When a long Saturn Line takes over a short Life Line at the base of the palm (Figure 9), you'll find a very busy person who's "gotta, gotta" get stuff done. The owner was "born with a briefcase." Early life was full of responsibility. Their middle name is "Work."

If this configuration is in your hands, people around you may wonder if you'll ever slow down and relax. You may find yourself sweeping the patio when there are no leaves to be found. If you don't have children of your own you'll find students or clients to take under your wing to nurture and mentor.

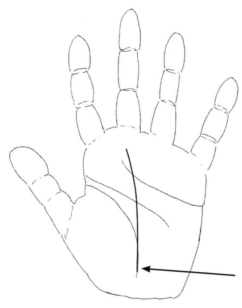

FIGURE 9: BUSY, BUSY

While I haven't seen a clear image of Margaret Thatcher's hands, in the series *The Crown* the prime minister said, "Work was our play. I'm not suited for time off; it gives me no pleasure." This is a common sentiment for someone with a Busy, Busy Fate Line.

This marking, and many others, are discussed in a more detail in my book, *Your Life Is In Your Hands: Practical Palm Reading for Purposeful Living*. But for now, if you own this marking, help others accept the notion that you are not meant to relax in the recliner because you're in go-mode, wired for work.

> STRENGTH: I take my duties seriously; I can be counted on and am determined to follow through.

> PITFALL: Compulsion to work.

> MONEY MINDSET: As a money machine, I consciously create balance in the massive amount of well-paid work I do, and I schedule well-deserved time to play.

> BREAKTHROUGH QUESTIONS: What if having unending undertakings was no longer important to me? How

would taking one day off a week serve my business and wellbeing? Is doing work for work's sake preventing me from applying my resources to financial payoff?

AFFIRMATION: "Fear and impatience demagnetize. Poise magnetizes." —Florence Scovel Shinn

Saturn Line Termination Points

Besides the origination point, the location on the hand where the Saturn Line stops provides a revealing indicator as to the Saturnian influence one will see in their life. The stopping point is usually in the upper half of the palm. The finger the Saturn Line ends under gives us clues about the associated interpretation. Let's find out what is meant by Saturn Lines ending in various areas of the palm.

Determined

In Figure 10, a long, straight vertical line starts at the base of the hand and rises all the way to the top of the palm, ending on the mount under the middle finger.

This long, straight Saturn Line indicates an organized person, with systems in place to complete tasks with flawless outcomes. In the positive, this person fulfills commitments and is driven by a thirst for knowledge. They are able to commit to a plan and follow through. On the negative side, this person may take on too much responsibility or feel overly obligated for the well-being of others resulting in diminished energy.

In the 2020 fall issue of *Onward*, the Charles Schwab investment publication, Schwab, founder and chairman, wrote, "The greater the challenge, the greater our resolve to come back stronger than before." He started the commentary with the year he was born—1937. Schwab has lived through financial crashes, pandemics, wars, the Great Depression, polio, the 9/11 terrorist attack and more. I haven't read his hands but I imagine the Saturn Line is long and well-marked in his hands. While not the best quality, a photo of his right hand I found on the Internet gives a reasonable impression of Schwab with a very long Fate Line.

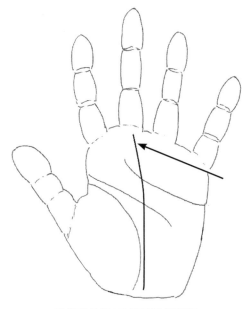

FIGURE 10: DETERMINED

STRENGTH: I am dogged, driven, focused and organized.

PITFALL: Excessive responsibility.

MONEY MINDSET: I am effectively aligned with successful outcomes to realize maximum riches.

BREAKTHROUGH QUESTIONS: Am I taking on responsibilities that aren't mine? If so, how would letting one or two of them go better support my wealth targets?

AFFIRMATION: "A winner never quits and a quitter never wins." —Anonymous

Super Responsible

When the Fate Line is straight, clear and extends up from the bottom center of the palm to the base of the Saturn finger (Figure 11), the owner is Super Responsible. This Saturn Line differs only slightly from Figure 10 (above) in that it reaches the base of the middle finger and can extend up into the finger.

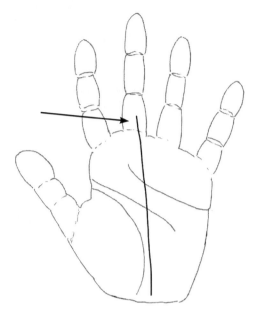

FIGURE II: SUPER RESPONSIBLE

The owner of this marking aims for and achieves A+ scores in many areas of life he or she focuses upon. Once a thing is decided upon the owner is typically unstoppable. They keep their pedal to the metal with clear direction and intent for nothing less than perfection. With a large and low set thumb (learn more in the chapter on thumbs) successful outcomes appear to come easily through having a larger territory. A smaller thumb, held naturally close to the palm, will be more comfortable being responsible within a smaller area to manage.

STRENGTH: Driven, dedicated, diligent, conscientious.

PITFALL: Serious and overly committed at the expense of personal relations.

MONEY MINDSET: With single-mindedness, I am unstoppable.

BREAKTHROUGH QUESTION: How can I be as committed to myself (and family) as I am to my projects and tasks?

AFFIRMATION: "All that is mine by Divine Right is now released and reaches me in great avalanches of abundance, under grace in miraculous ways." —Florence Scovel Shinn

Driven to Influence

You are a man or woman of powerful influence if either of your hands has a Saturn Line stretching from the lower area of the palm up toward your pointer finger (Figure 12). Claim your natural inclination to show the way.

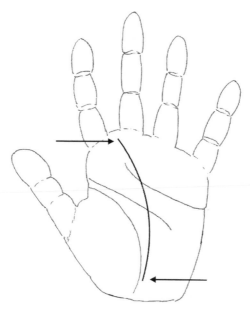

FIGURE 12: DRIVEN TO INFLUENCE

This is a combination of Saturn representing duty and value, with Jupiter, the pointer finger, showing the urge to lead and direct. When the Saturn Line climbs up with this trajectory, I read the owner as having torrential drive.

An image I found of Arnold Schwarzenegger's right hand shows this configuration. Schwarzenegger, actor and 38th governor of California, moved to the U.S. from Austria, became Mr. Universe and Mr. Olympia besides a lead actor in the films *Terminator* and *Twins*.

This line indicates the need to be queen or king. If you have this etching, find your right territory with ideal followers. Ideal followers are those interested in your vision and why you're motivated toward that vision. If you have overbearing tendencies, keep your sight on the highest good of the individuals who need a leader, and that's you!

STRENGTH: With clarity of vision, I am a groundbreaker leading the way.

PITFALL: Pushiness, or trying to be friends with followers.

MONEY MINDSET: With reclaimed power and confidence I eagerly show the way for the highest good of all concerned—and I am financially triumphant.

BREAKTHROUGH QUESTIONS: Am I open to the possibility that someone may not like me but respects the direction I give for the greater good? What unpopular decision have I recently made that was for the betterment of the whole tribe/family? How might my bank account increase if I take a risk to stand out in front and lead others more frequently?

AFFIRMATION: "Sure-ism is stronger than optimism."
—Florence Scovel Shin

Shine

When the Saturn Line rises from the lower area of the palm and veers toward the ring finger (Figure 13), we'll discover a highly creative individual with impulse to sparkle in the spotlight.

The ring finger is called Apollo in Palmese. Read more about Apollo in the chapter about fingers, middle finger sections and finger spacing. Apollo was born to be seen and applauded. If you have this imprint in your hand, you are driven to achieve in the arts. This configuration indicates a non-negotiable urge to create. If you don't think of yourself as an artist, think again. Do you improvise when "following" a recipe? Do you give the kids or friends imaginative ways to solve problems? Are you inspired to form something where there was

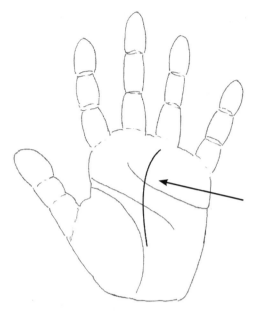

FIGURE 13: SHINE

nothing before? Don't underestimate your knack for resourceful and inventive ways. Notice how the effort you put forth transmutes into unique outcomes. Remember, creative types *do* make money. Identify role models who shine in the spotlight and inquire about their success strategies and mindsets.

> STRENGTH: I am highly creative, express myself freely and approve of myself—fully and completely.
>
> PITFALL: Paralyzing fear of rejection.
>
> MONEY MINDSET: I am committed to allowing my authentic and inventive self to shine in all areas of my life, including wildly successful money-making endeavors.
>
> BREAKTHROUGH QUESTIONS: If failure was not an option, what would I say "yes" to? If disapproval was no longer important to me, what or whom would I say "no" to?
>
> AFFIRMATION: "I am now linked by an invisible, unbreakable magnetic cord with all that belongs to me by Divine Right!" —Florence Scovel Shin

For Love's Sake

When the Saturn Line rises upward and stops at the Heart Line (Figure 14) the owner is known to quit a job for the sake of love. Career goals, studies and responsibilities are rearranged for love.

If you have this design in either of your hands, your love life interferes with your aspirations. You care deeply and want to please your mate even if that means the grand gesture of changing careers after you spent years in college getting the degree for your dream job. After redirecting your efforts toward a "more acceptable" career with your mate in mind, you may find yourself once again quitting to keep him or her happy. Be conscious of your past choices for money *or* relationship. You can make both happen but it will first require self-love and honest communication with yourself and your mate.

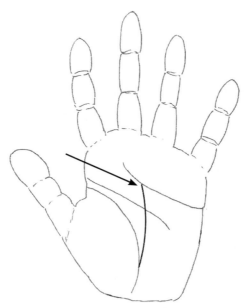

FIGURE 14: FOR LOVE'S SAKE

One of my clients whose Saturn Line stopped at the Heart Line met her husband at work. After fifteen years they're still married. Another client whose Saturn Line stopped at the Heart Line changed his career twice over the course of twenty years in an attempt to keep his mate satisfied. They're no longer married.

STRENGTH: I care deeply and am joyful as I choose for love.

PITFALL: Aimless in the name of relationship.

MONEY MINDSET: I balance my want for relationship and self-worth with choices to create more money.

BREAKTHROUGH QUESTION: What actions would I take if I were committed to being the best at what I do?

AFFIRMATION: "I give thanks that the marriage made in heaven is now made manifest upon earth." —Florence Scovel Shinn

Mickey Mouse Details

When the Saturn Line stops at the Head Line (Figure 15), we catch a person who finds themselves perplexed by unexpected details, derailing their activities to finish a project. Richard Unger named this configuration Mickey Mouse Details because of the intrusion of things requiring thoughts (Head Line) while the owner is on task (Saturn Line), aimed toward a particular outcome.

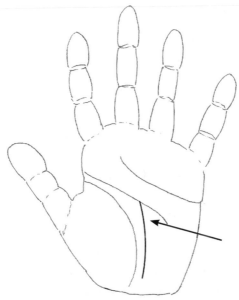

FIGURE 15: MICKEY MOUSE DETAILS

Watch how your revenue-generating genius and jobs becomes de-railed by things such as your new phone not working and needs to be returned, a required computer update unexpectedly taking four hours to install or a software glitch resulting in loss of all data—poof! Hire experts to shore up your detail-required jobs that pull you away from essential money-generating priorities—and be sure to have priorities in the first place. If you don't identify priorities, the Mikey Mouse details will become your priorities.

> STRENGTH: I am an expert at solving problems, I discern wisely to delegate where possible, while staying focused to complete my current project.

> PITFALL: Interruptions create unmanageable frustration, which triggers project abort, boredom.

> MONEY MINDSET: I keep my cool and get back on track after the interruptions are effectively and swiftly handled by me or someone else.

> BREAKTHROUGH QUESTIONS: How can I best apply myself to current circumstances? How will my project(s) benefit as I find ways to delegate problem-solving? What's my secret sauce for completing jobs on time, with grace and ease?

> AFFIRMATION: "I am unmoved by appearances, therefore appearances move." —Florence Scovel Shinn

Think of the lines in the hands as electrical wiring, allowing currents of energy to flow. The longer the line, the farther the energy is conveyed. Clearer lines indicate energy flowing more effectively. Shorter lines run energy for shorter periods of time. The condition of the finger the Saturn Line is aiming toward is also significant, as will be discussed in the chapter on fingers. For example, the straighter the finger above the end of a Saturn Line, the better and more positively the associated characteristics of the finger will be realized and expressed. At least, there is a potential for greater expression.

Following are more Saturn Line configurations. Take a look at your hands, and hands of friends, family and co-workers, to train your eye and practice speaking about what you're learning. Experiment!

Saturn Line Variations

Variety

Multiple short vertical lines on the mount under the middle finger (Figure 16) indicates a person continually contemplating a variety of careers to pursue. He or she is most likely a master multitasker able to juggle an assortment of assignments.

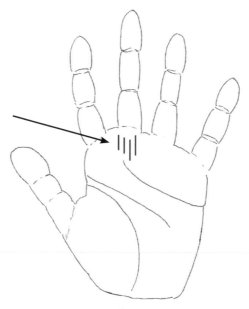

FIGURE 16: VARIETY

However, if money is your objective and you have stretched yourself too thin, then give yourself permission to choose your top one or two priorities each week. Ask yourself, "What's important about having all of these tasks, responsibilities and commitments?" To become more mindful, and therefore able to best manage your time, getting to the root of the exacerbated rain of responsibilities will be helpful. Mental patterns have been constructed including career attention aimed in a wide range of directions. Becoming conscious is key and will lead to balance and ease.

STRENGTH: An array of interests keep me stimulated.

PITFALL: Stretched too thin.

MONEY MINDSET: Each week I identify my #1 top revenue-generating task and I commit fully to seeing it through while relishing my success.

BREAKTHROUGH QUESTIONS: What work story am I telling myself? What work story do I want to be true? What must be true to complete my #1 top revenue-generating task this week?

AFFIRMATION: "I am linked with an endless golden stream of prosperity which comes to me under grace in perfect ways." —Florence Scovel Shin

Scattered

Somewhat similar to the previous illustration, Figure 17 shows several vertical lines starting lower on the palm, climbing upward toward the middle finger. Multiple overlapping vertical lines indicate determination with a strong tendency to take on many projects.

The good news is that this person has plenty of drive. The bad news is that this person may have too many projects going on at the same time, with none getting finished, resulting in a feeling of inadequacy. The owner of multiple Saturn Lines is challenged to commit to one project and follow it through to completion.

Several vertical lines climbing toward the middle finger signify being divided between many endeavors. For example, one may be writing a cookbook, a parenting book and rebuilding a 1966 Mustang. As a result, attention is scattered and either the projects take a very long time to complete or none get completed at all.

If you own this line pattern and you truly feel good about the multiplicity, then be happy with that. Find the core of yourself in each endeavor. Replace feelings of guilt and inadequacy with confidence and joy in your efforts. However, if money is something you want more of and you acknowledge your habit of "project dance" or "job hop," then make an intention to create new habits to discern, focus and finish. Complete projects, programs, tasks and jobs that generate revenue.

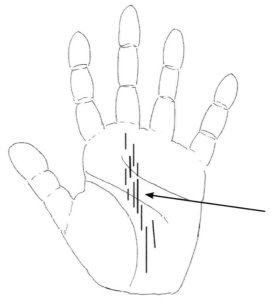

FIGURE 17: SCATTERED

STRENGTH: Variety of skills and interests make me knowledgeable.

PITFALL: Difficulty finishing what was started.

MONEY MINDSET: I am conscious of where I put my commitments and I stay on track, achieving outstanding results, receiving enormous financial reward.

BREAKTHROUGH QUESTION: Out of all the choices I have for making money, which will I remain most committed to for the long haul?

AFFIRMATION: "I now release the gold mine within me." —Florence Scovel Shinn

Career Cracks and Opportunities

When the Saturn Line begins near the base of the hand, starts its climb, stops and shifts to one side, starts, then stops again, with another shift back and repeats itself, you'll find someone who loses direction at various times throughout life. For example, a commitment is made to

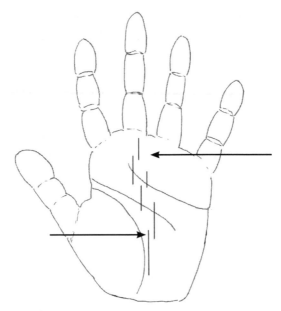

FIGURE 18: CAREER CRACKS AND OPPORTUNITIES

study biology. After graduation the commitment changes to starting a food truck business. Later, direction is shifted to volunteering at the zoo. Next comes a drive for directing a non-profit organization.

Gaps between the starting and stopping points indicate feeling lost for a short time. Overlaps between the two Fate Lines indicates temporarily doing two jobs or projects at the same time before completely picking up with the new endeavor. Don't let judgments about your job/project/direction changes defeat you. Career cracks can offer career opportunities.

> STRENGTH: I am committed to the task at hand and feel extraordinarily accomplished.
>
> PITFALL: Feelings of inadequacy or defeat with each ending and starting all over—again.
>
> MONEY MINDSET: I see the good in who I am and eagerly apply myself right where I am. Results in revenue are definite.

BREAKTHROUGH QUESTIONS: If I were to choose again, what new choice would I make? What outcome do I foresee if I stay the course instead of changing?

AFFIRMATION: "The genius within me is now released. I now fulfill my destiny." —Florence Scovel Shinn

Commitment Issues

With two Saturn Lines running parallel between 1/8 and 1/2 inch up the center of the hand, the owner will grapple with commitment issues between two endeavors *or* relish in the dedication toward two paths of attention. The length of these vertical parallel lines can be short or long.

For example, if you own this configuration, you may find yourself dedicated to two different careers such as a corporate job and a side business in the healing arts. Another case is having a passion to write a series of books while also managing vacation rentals. You may find yourself feeling less than content because you're doing one thing when you want to be doing the other. Perhaps one line of work is bringing in the money while the other is most desired for inner fulfillment.

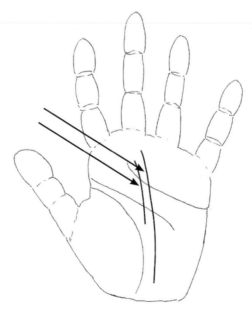

FIGURE 19: COMMITMENT ISSUES

STRENGTH: I am advancing in two lines of work and developing titanic skills.

PITFALL: Internal division, feeling unfulfilled.

MONEY MINDSET: I accept and appreciate how I apply myself as I align with each project or job and charge what I'm worth in both.

BREAKTHROUGH QUESTIONS: What mindset would best serve me in using my time efficiently and without guilt? What's in conflict for me regarding these two career/work/project paths? Is there a new decision I'd like to make? If so, what is it?

AFFIRMATION: "Divine ideas never conflict." —Florence Scovel Shinn

Hard Work

When two Fate Lines closely parallel within about 1/16 inch up the center of the palm (Figure 20), you'll find someone working hard for some period of time. The length of time depends on the distance the two lines are parallel. The further they travel together up the center of the hand, the longer the owner will be running hard. For example, the person could be working by day and attending school at night. Or he or she could be taking care of the kids during the day and developing websites in early morning and late-night hours, too.

A common money-making myth is "To make more money, I must work harder and longer." I ask, "Is that true?" The answer is no. However, the owner of this configuration very well could be burning the candle at both ends. His or her aim is powered by money, habit, compulsion or conscious fulfillment.

STRENGTH: I'm on fire!

PITFALL: Unexpected burnout.

MONEY MINDSET: I use my workhorse capabilities to achieve maximum result and return on investment, while honoring my need to rest—a bit.

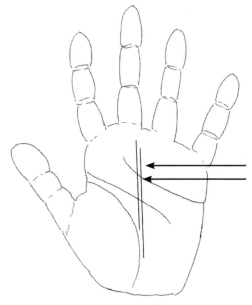

FIGURE 20: HARD WORK

BREAKTHROUGH QUESTIONS: Am I deciding against myself in any area of my life? If so, where, and what decision will I make about it? What if I could generate more wealth while working less?

AFFIRMATION: "My money works hard for me and makes me more and more money." —T. Harv Eker

There are many possibilities for Saturn Line configurations. The key to interpreting the line is to note where the line starts and stops, because the meaning associated with those areas are blended together to formulate an interpretation.

Heart and Fate Line Intersections

Take particular interest when the Heart Line and the Fate Line join in some way. The Heart Line is read to interpret a person's emotional style, which is endlessly engaged throughout the day. The Fate Line relates to work. Blend the meaning of the Fate Line and Heart Line and decipher the recipe for emotional involvement and response at work.

Love of Work

When the Saturn Line climbs from the lower area of the palm and merges with the Heart Line (Figure 21), you'll find someone with a non-negotiable, deep passion for work. The emotional system thrives through task, effort and one-pointed direction. Ideally the owner has a career to pour herself into, spending countless hours ambitiously engaged in projects.

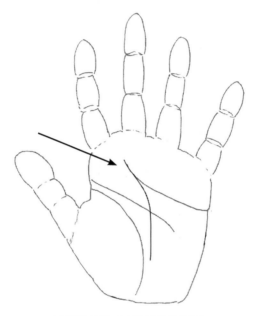

FIGURE 21: LOVE OF WORK

If this design is in your hands, people may call you a workaholic—and you accept the compliment. Indulging in your ravenous love of effort makes you happy. Accomplishment is a value held near and dear to your heart, especially if you have a strong thumb type (see the chapter on thumbs). You're committed to getting it done with love and zeal. However, ask yourself, "Is there any of me left over for partnership?"

> STRENGTH: I absolutely love the work I do and I'm unstoppable!

> PITFALL: Difficulties in personal relationships, neglecting health.

MONEY MINDSET: While I am passionate about my work, I take good care of myself as well as others. I love money and money loves me.

BREAKTHROUGH QUESTIONS: What is one baby step I will take to balance my health and well-being with my insatiable love of work? Will I look back and have any regrets?

AFFIRMATION: "I now let go of worn-out conditions and worn-out things." —Florence Scovel Shin

Project Loyalty

When the Saturn Line stops the Heart Line (Figure 22), you'll find someone whose affections are interrupted by their career activities. A short Heart Line belongs to someone who must produce, like the Earth producing crops. (Read more about the Hermit—Independent Heart Line in the chapter on Heart Lines.) Combine the high productivity requirements of the short Heart Line with the drive of the long Saturn

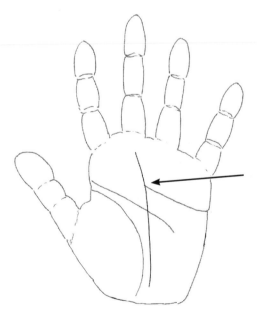

FIGURE 22: PROJECT LOYALTY

Line appearing to stop the Heart Line, and we have a double dose of devotion and attention to the mission.

If this design is impressed into either of your hands, you are self-reliant, dedicated and disciplined in the direction of what is most important to you. Being out of balance is the downside possibility. For example, are you about all work and no play? If you're in a relationship with a significant other, how's life in the department of closeness and affection? It's most likely you've successfully set up your life for sanctuary, safety and work, with less importance put on a special relationship. If you are in a special connection and you're free to work as you wish, then you'll be loyal until the end of time.

STRENGTH: Assigned allegiance is the truest desire of my heart.

PITFALL: Reluctant communications around emotions.

MONEY MINDSET: I stretch myself through uncomfortable change and am open to unlimited possibilities as a dedicated money machine.

BREAKTHROUGH QUESTION: How could taking a little more time to communicate with a business or love partner increase my bank balance?

AFFIRMATION: Exceeding expectations at work and in relationship comes easily to me.

My Money Map Exercise

Using the words in this book, describe the strengths and pitfalls linked to your Fate Lines, if you find any, in either or both hands. Also note the associated Money Mindsets. (See the example on page 60.)

The Fate Line Types I See in My Hands

Right Hand

PAGE: _____ MARKING: _____

STRENGTH: _____

_____

PITFALL: _____

_____

MONEY MINDSET: _____

_____

_____

Left Hand

PAGE: _____ MARKING: _____

STRENGTH: _____

_____

PITFALL: _____

_____

MONEY MINDSET: _____

_____

_____

*Note the markings you see in both hands on the blank
hand maps at the back of this book, pages 212–213.*

Example

The Fate Line Types I See in My Hands

Right Hand

PAGE: <u>31</u> MARKING: <u>Intuitively Guided</u>

STRENGTH: <u>My intuition is sharp and accurate. I never</u>
<u>argue with a hunch.</u>

PITFALL: <u>Relying too much on logic and reason.</u>

_____

MONEY MINDSET: <u>I am in the right place at the right time</u>
<u>to engage in inspirational and meaningful work both to</u>
<u>give and receive prosperity.</u>

Left Hand

PAGE: <u>38</u> MARKING: <u>Busy, Busy</u>

STRENGTH: <u>I take my duties seriously; I can be counted on</u>
<u>and am determined to follow through.</u>

PITFALL: <u>Compulsion to work</u>

_____

MONEY MINDSET: <u>As a money machine, I consciously create</u>
<u>balance in the massive amount of well-paid work I do, and</u>
<u>I schedule well-deserved time to play.</u>

Note the markings you see in both hands
on the blank hand maps at the back of this book, pages 212–213.

Challenge Markings

How to Overcome These Obstacles to Financial Freedom

> *"I am not afraid. I was born to do this."*
> —*Joan of Arc*

NOW YOU'LL BE introduced to a few Challenge Markings (Figure 23) in the hands. These patterns typically imply significant difficulties for people with any of these markings. However, the owner of one or more of the Challenge Markings may not see a recurring problem as difficult to deal with because he or she is accustomed to carrying that burden through life—day in and day out. The negative patterns feel like a dull pain or subtle irritation but not always painful enough to change.

You'll now learn how to clearly recognize specific markings in the hands that denote unmistakable obstacles to financial freedom and living a more fulfilling life. This is where shifting your mindsets is crucial. What's really noteworthy is how a string of Challenge Markings can point you directly to critical pieces of the puzzle causing the most frustration. Now you'll become better equipped to manage the fragments and actually learn valuable lessons because of what they reveal in your life. Stay open and receptive, being present right where the creative tension is, where the tightness of the life challenges are—or appear to be. Think of the Challenge Markings as powerful growth markings providing reliable signposts to ignite both personal and professional growth.

Take note of what you learn in the following pages related to Challenge Markings you may find in your hands. If you have any, do com-

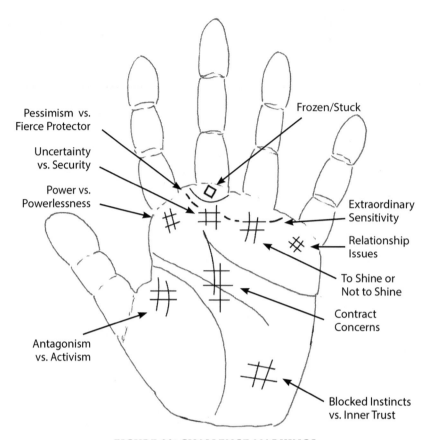

Pessimism vs.
Fierce Protector

Uncertainty
vs. Security

Power vs.
Powerlessness

Frozen/Stuck

Extraordinary
Sensitivity

Relationship
Issues

To Shine or
Not to Shine

Contract
Concerns

Antagonism
vs. Activism

Blocked Instincts
vs. Inner Trust

FIGURE 23: CHALLENGE MARKINGS

plete the My Money Map Exercise at the end of the chapter. Make these assignments work for you and your future.

Grills can appear in many areas of the hand. What they're about and where they're located will tell the significance of the glyphs. Grills are formed by crossing horizontal and vertical lines like a hashtag or tic-tac-toe as shown in the figure above. The horizontal lines represent blockage and the vertical lines signify flow. Have you ever followed behind a car driving uphill with the brake lights on? The driver has one foot on the gas and the other on the brakes. Extra fuel is required to drive to the top of the hill, or anywhere for that matter.

Jupiter Grill—Power vs. Powerlessness

A grill on the mount just under the base of the index finger, relates to Jupiter behaviors. The stop-and-go effect leads to confusion around ambitions and/or authority. Power giveaway is a distinct possibility with this inscription.

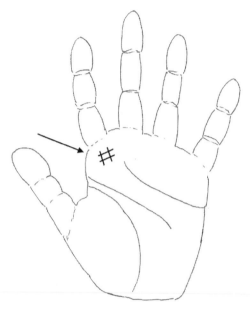

FIGURE 24: POWER VS. POWERLESSNESS

These vertical lines indicate ability to make positive and powerful decisions. However, struggles ensue as another person, thing or organization strives for command over you and your decision-making. The topic often involves what you feel passionate about, how you want to pursue your ambitions, what inspires you. With business, work and money decisions, take strong inventory of how and whom you give your power to. Draw forth your power scepter and reclaim your power for prosperity. To build up your strength, practice describing what you want to close friends, in a journal or to your pet.

STRENGTH: My ability is strong for making powerful decisions.

PITFALL: Authority tug-of-war.

MONEY MINDSET: My power scepter wields focus and muscle to achieve my financial goals.

BREAKTHROUGH QUESTIONS: In what ways have I lost economically by giving my power away? What would I do differently next time? What are my top three "I wants," and whose permission do I need to attain them?

AFFIRMATION: "I am stronger than I believe. I have greater power than I know." —Wonder Woman

Saturn Grill—Uncertainty vs. Security

We'll now look at the push-and-pull effect related to responsibility, work, focus, values and money represented by your middle finger.

If you have the tic-tac-toe symbol on the mount under your middle finger (Figure 25), you'll experience snags "fighting against" and at the same time experience "yes" movement in the area of responsibilities, rules, values, agreements and money. In short: money issues. Your aim is security. With financial security a sense of confidence follows. This confidence leads you firmly on your path to what you value.

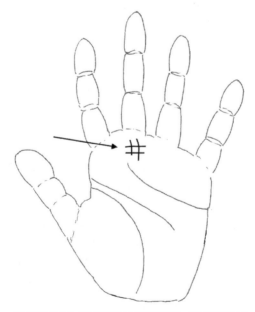

FIGURE 25: UNCERTAINTY VS. SECURITY

This symbol is a call for clarity around what you deem important. For example, where do you want your four-year-old to attend preschool? What are your values around birth control? What is your moral code when it comes to war and peace? Grappling with issues of value must be addressed head-on to alleviate insecurities. Do you need to have a tough conversation with your mate or business partner involving your values, morals and how you choose to commit yourself (or not) to a project, line of work or business practice?

> STRENGTH: Contrast and uncertainty ignite clarity and alignment for what I want and why I want it.

> PITFALL: Constant fighting within myself.

> MONEY MINDSET: I carve out the time I need to align with "yes" movement and focus plans toward my financial goals.

> BREAKTHROUGH QUESTIONS: What one thing do I grapple with and fight against, more than anything else, that needs resolution? While experiencing money issues with someone, what's most important to me that's not understood by the other person? Is what I believe to be so important really *that* important? What do I stand for no matter what?

> AFFIRMATION: The tide of Destiny has turned and everything comes my way. —Florence Scovel Shinn

Diamond or Box on the Saturn Mount— Frozen/Stuck

A diamond on the Saturn Line on the Saturn Mount (Figure 26) is a sign of feeling frozen. Similarly, a box on the Saturn Mount (Figure 27) indicates feeling stuck. Because both involve a Saturnian area of the palm, circumstances will involve money, time, commitments, work etc. For example, either marking might relate to assets that you value being tied up and unavailable (stuck or frozen) for use. Conversely, things you no longer value are holding you back. The length of time for the dilemma would be unknown but because the mark is visible, either the thought, concern or physical circumstance is likely to be present.

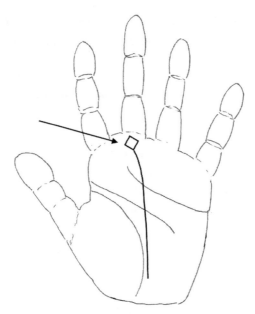

FIGURE 26: FROZEN

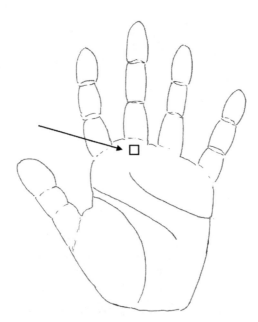

FIGURE 27: STUCK

Boxes also indicate feelings of being boxed in, for example, being locked into an unwanted job for whatever reason, or, conversely, not being able to find a job no matter how hard the owner searches. With either a diamond or box in this location, the owner will find many reasons for their predicament of feeling ensnared, trapped and stifled.

STRENGTH: I now see this plight of feeling locked in and assert my determination to make powerful changes in my life starting today.

PITFALL: Endless excuses for being stuck; ineffectiveness.

MONEY MINDSET: With a solid plan I take baby steps forward into new, unexplored directions, committing to new tasks to create colossal amounts of cash. I don't give up.

BREAKTHROUGH QUESTIONS: Is being stuck serving me in any way? If I were guaranteed to never run out of money, what would I change in my life? Is it time to let go of anything or anyone in my life?

AFFIRMATION: "I make friends with hindrances and every obstacle becomes a stepping-stone." —Florence Scovel Shinn

Contract Concerns

When a grill or ladder joins with the Heart Line under the middle finger (Figure 28), the owner will clash with loved ones regarding contracts and agreements. Loved ones can include family members, friends, business partners and clients.

This configuration indicates uncertainties about values and money within a relationship. Fighting both internally and externally about tasks, moral alliances, rules and commitments is common in relationships. For example, is it important or not for bills to be paid on time? Is it okay to be late to meetings? What are the policies in your business related to refunds or returns? A handshake may be enough to seal the deal for the owner of this ladder, but is it for the person on the other side of the grip?

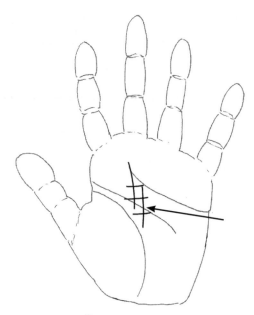

FIGURE 28: CONTRACT CONCERNS

If you own this marking, notice when you experience repeated disappointment with what you deem irresponsible behavior of people in your life. The challenge for you is to impose consequences with certain people who don't honor your rules. Hold your own. Keep your half of the contract, especially during emotional disruption. Nurture respect and integrity in relationships that are important to you and carve out time to clarify your rules, even if it's difficult at first. Listening with an open mind and seeing the other person's perspective will help during challenging conversations.

> STRENGTH: Using disagreement to get clear, and speaking up about what's significant to me for the health of the partnership.

> PITFALL: Retreat into low self-esteem, feeling disappointment in others and self.

> MONEY MINDSET: I love myself enough to say what I want and consistently fortify contracts with care.

BREAKTHROUGH QUESTIONS: Is it time to stop loaning money to a loved one when I know they won't pay it back? What would make it easier to discuss the details of agreements with my important partners? If I have experienced disappointment in a broken agreement in the past, what will I do differently in the future?

AFFIRMATION: "Behold! I have set before thee the open door of Destiny and no man (or woman) shall shut it, for it is *nailed back.*" —Florence Scovel Shinn

Ring of Saturn—Pessimism vs. Fierce Protector

To find the Ring of Saturn look underneath the middle finger on the Saturn Mount. This is an uncommon marking to find in the hand. It resembles a half-circle or an open bucket (Figure 29). A solid-lined ring will be most challenging, but the potency is decreased when the bucket is "stitched in."

This ring acts as a barrier to the continuity of the energy or current running through the finger. On the down side, the ring shuts out an advanced Saturn quality—wisdom. With this energy in jeopardy the owner may hop around from job to job because he or she is lacking in direction. Look to the thumb (in a following chapter) for positive or negative support.

The sense of long-term isolation is not uncommon with this rare Challenge Marking. He or she thinks, "I'm all alone in this abysmal world." In secret, he or she feels scared because things are getting worse and worse. They're prone to overreact to what may appear threatening. Alternatively, the owner acts with bravado, portraying "nothing scares me."

Did you see the film *Conspiracy Theory* with Mel Gibson and Julia Roberts? The film centers on an eccentric taxi driver in New York City (Gibson) who is absolutely convinced many world events are triggered by government conspiracies. The plot never discloses what is true and what isn't.

On the upside, the owner of a Ring of Saturn demonstrates appropriate discretion. He or she always has a Plan "B." The owner understands other people's pessimism. They have an inside voice of caution.

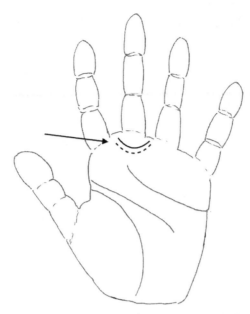

FIGURE 29: PESSIMISM VS. FIERCE PROTECTOR

Their doubt and skepticism operate in a more constructive way when they don't get stuck in suspicion. They have a healthy outlet for preparedness. Potential positions could include a Red Cross leader who is trained to "be prepared," a drill sergeant shaping civilians into the best soldiers in the world or a Secret Service agent assigned to protect political leaders and their families.

This is someone who does well planning for and preventing bomb threats, terrorist attacks or computer hacking. At their best they transform paralyzing fear and pessimism into performance as fierce protectors.

> STRENGTH: I consider every possible scenario and keep people safe and secure.

> PITFALL: Drowning in suspicion, feeling alone and isolated.

> MONEY MINDSET: My intelligence is highly valued for safety and security, and I am handsomely paid. Isn't money wonderful?

BREAKTHROUGH QUESTIONS: What is frugality or fear keeping me from doing or becoming? How can I use my "Here's Plan 'B'" expertise to generate greater wealth? Where would my consulting skills be best utilized and recognized?

AFFIRMATION: "I am awake to my good, and gather in the harvest of endless opportunities." —Florence Scovel Shinn

Apollo Grill—To Shine or Not to Shine

Look for crossing horizontal and vertical lines like a tic-tac-toe on the mount under the Apollo (ring) finger (Figure 30). Horizontal lines rep-

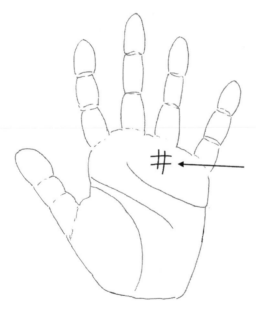

FIGURE 30: TO SHINE OR NOT TO SHINE?

resent blockage and vertical lines signify flow. This push and pull leads to back-and-forth movement between apathy and creativity—doubt and fear involving one's unique talents.

If you feel a compulsion to express something big and this tic-tac-toe is sketched onto your Apollo Mount, don't despair. Think of this as an opportunity to overcome and build unstoppable energy and strength to express that special something that will definitely benefit someone or multitudes. Imagine how your fulfillment factor will magnify when you feel the fear and blast through it!

> STRENGTH: Regardless of killjoys, I am in touch with and emanate *that* creative expression designed into my soul that has chosen me to live through!

> PITFALL: Doubt, apprehension, starving artist syndrome.

> MONEY MINDSET: Through experimentation and play I find my way to create; my bank account grows by leaps and bounds!

> BREAKTHROUGH QUESTIONS: If I no longer gave power to anyone (or anything) to reject my true essence and what I'm here to do, what changes would I make and by when? If doubt disappeared and was no longer part of my make-up (poof, gone!) how would my one-of-a-kind essence shine through?

> AFFIRMATION: "I banish the past and now live in the wonderful now, where happy surprises come to me each day." —Florence Scovel Shinn

Mercury Grill—Relationship Issues

A hashtag mark on the mount under the pinkie finger signifies communication blocks. At the owner's best, he or she is tuned in to his or her inner voice and follows it appropriately. But the horizontal lines indicate resistance to speaking up, withholding or ignoring the inner voice. This in turn creates internal doubt and trust issues.

If you find this etching in your hand, ask yourself what you're not hearing. Listening to one's self takes great courage. It's often easier to listen to, and believe in, what others say. This is a call to tune in to your inner messaging system and speak up. Imagine how your relationships will improve—with your mate, boss, business partner and financial advisor.

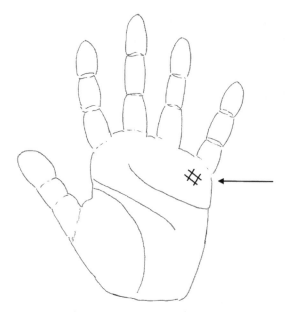

FIGURE 31: RELATIONSHIP ISSUES

STRENGTH: My inner messaging system is amplified, transmitted and received.

PITFALL: Distrust, silent when it's time to speak up.

MONEY MINDSET: The value and volume of my voice fills my velvet purse with endless supply.

BREAKTHROUGH QUESTIONS: While I am trustworthy, where is a lack of trust preventing me from saying "yes" to opportunities for creating wealth? How is believing I won't be heard holding me back? What needs to be said, and to whom, today?

AFFIRMATION: "Speaking confidently is the most natural thing in the world." —Trinity Affirmations

Mars Grill—Antagonism vs. Activism

When a grill or a ladder is stamped into the area just inside the start of the Life Line, on the Mars Mount (Figure 32), the owner will grapple with feelings ranging from hostility to heroism.

In Greek mythology, goddess Hera didn't like the fact that Zeus, her husband, had a baby with another woman, so she had serpents sent to kill the illegitimate baby Hercules in his cradle. Hercules and Mars are two different characters, but both express in-built strength and protection of those unable to stand up for themselves. Upon sight of the serpents, Hercules choked them to death. Hence, this area of the hand relates to courage.

The tic-tac-toe effect blocks the healthy flow of energy, which in turn creates a sense of antagonism that resembles a chip on the shoulder. This interference can also emerge in one's life as grievances,

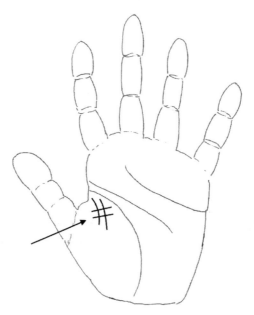

FIGURE 32: ANTAGONISM VS. ACTIVISM

injustices, victimization and criticism of others or self. One client told me, "My father didn't acknowledge me for the causes I stood for, so I dismissed him from my life."

In the positive, we find characters like action figure Xena the Warrior Princess, who uses her fighting skills to help people. Owners of this grill need to be involved with a worthy crusade, otherwise the energy will fire-hose in negative directions.

STRENGTH: I stand strong in my fight for injustice and prevail with courage and character.

PITFALL: Hostility and quarrelsomeness restrict participation as an effective team player.

MONEY MINDSET: With astounding strength for worthy causes, I make an impact in the world and I'm richly rewarded.

BREAKTHROUGH QUESTIONS: Is there someone in my life whom I still hold a grudge against that if I were to let it go, I'd have even more energy for positive use? As a mighty advocate for action, how can I best handle a current conflict?

AFFIRMATION: "There are no obstacles in Divine Mind, therefore, there is nothing to obstruct my good." —Florence Scovel Shinn

Moon Grill or Horizontal— Blocked Instincts vs. Inner Truth

When a grill, large or small, is found on the Moon Mount (Figure 33), you'll find crisis of meaning in the owner's psychological makeup. "What is the best way to live a meaningful life?" or "Is it even possible to live a meaningful life in this upside-down world?" are thoughts he or she will wrestle with fairly often.

The Moon Mount is read to see how a person tunes in to his or her instinctual nature. This section of the hand relates to our core identity—how we see ourselves as individuals relative to others. If I ask you, "Who do you take yourself to be?" you'd reply with your identification with being, for example, a loner, loser, go-getter, hard worker, writer, loved, unloved etc. Core fears, hurts and dreams are, in a sense, stored in the Moon Mount. Therapists, counselors and coaches guide us into this area of our lives to help increase self-worth and pursue our dreams, but this requires vulnerability and a desire to explore our interior selves.

The owner of a grill in the Moon Mount does want to know why she's here and how to make her best contribution to the world. The problem presents itself through (1) not having help to reflect on and overcome sources of grief, and (2) resistance to knowing her purpose for fear of potential change. The second is most often encountered with a single horizontal line crossing through the Moon Mount.

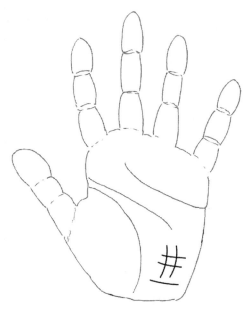

FIGURE 33: BLOCKED INSTINCTS VS. INNER TRUST

STRENGTH: With love of myself, I consistently tune in and awaken my innermost truth.

PITFALL: Extended isolation, anxiety, disconnection from one's inner nature.

MONEY MINDSET: My lively imagination and deep thoughts about the meaning of life are put to wholesome use in an environment that pays exceptionally well.

BREAKTHROUGH QUESTIONS: What if needing certain people's approval about living my desired dreams and purpose, was no longer important to me? Is there a memory I haven't explored from all directions, that if I did, would free me from sadness? How might making regular entries into a day/night dream journal serve me in living a life with more meaning?

AFFIRMATION: "Divine order is established in my mind, body and affairs." —Florence Scovel Shinn

Overall, grills dampen the ability to reach goals and achieve success until one knows how to work with the trials indicated for the owner. It's important to be equipped to handle the hurdles and overcome the obstacles.

Girdle of Venus—Extraordinary Sensitivity

The Girdle of Venus illustrates remarkable—and oftentimes over-whelming—atunement to the widespread energy patterns surround-ing the owner. One line or multiple lines may form a bowl-like pattern below the middle and ring fingers on the upper area of the palm, above the Heart Line (Figure 34).

Excessive feelings, sympathies and overwhelming emotions will most likely be found in the life of the owner with this marking. Imagine a village of senses housed within a person. All the individual senses are the villagers pushing about on a highly energetic superhighway.

When interpreted, the Heart Line (discussed in a later chapter) describes a person's emotional style: the lovability and non-negotiable relationship requirements. The Girdle of Venus is a sister line, assisting the energy of the Heart Line to expand and intensify the emotional system.

If you own a Girdle of Venus, at your best you are nurturing, affec-tionate, warm, friendly and compassionate, with a heightened sense of imagination and intense sensitivity to suffering. When you are triggered by something saddening and a response of disappointment, despair or overwhelming emotion develops, you can easily launch into negative characteristics. At your worst you become depressive and paralyzed by what you perceive to be happening around you. You can make moun-tains out of molehills, escape into substances (like drugs and alcohol) and useless fantasy. With conscious attention and a trustworthy tool-kit, you can move beyond the behaviors on the negative side over to the positive. The first step is to notice the response, triggered by the upset, and choose which direction to move toward, positive or negative. A reaction is a pointer, like a road sign, that a choice is to be made.

If you have this marking, you may have learned to manage your

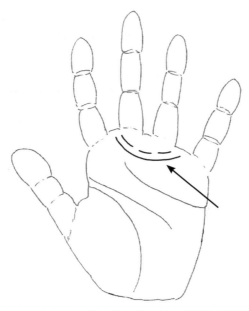

FIGURE 34: EXTRAORDINARY SENSITIVITY

profound sensitivity to suffering and sadness with earmuffs (invisible or visible). Ear protection is symbolic for much-needed protection from wide-scale energies that can be exceedingly overwhelming. The sensation of misery, agony and torment can feel unbearable. In reaction to this subtle and usually indescribable agitation, you may have chosen to live in the country or along the open coastline, away from the pinball energy of the city. Or perhaps you go on regular retreats if you reside in the urban realms. Ideally, you walk with care to protect your village of senses.

It's very important to care for yourself and the effects of the invisible antennas permanently mounted to the top of your head. You are in constant contact, tuned in, tapped in and turned on to subtle energies at a universal level. Build in regular and healthy "get-aways."

If you seek for understanding from a friend or mate, don't be disappointed when he or she changes the subject as you acknowledge your heartache. People without these lines (or other sensitivity markings) are most likely unable to comprehend the energetic affects you experience.

At your very best you will harness the elevated vision you carry with your faith in the divine and fully utilize your experience and skill working for universal welfare. Perhaps you choose to perform as a deeply caring nurse, nutrition coach, wellness advisor, social worker, hospice worker, green peace worker or some spiritual function help-ing at a worldly level. Hand analysis, quantum healing, yoga, world wide meditation circles, Habitat for Humanity, emotional freedom techniques and other metaphysical fields bring out the psychology of the heart. On the master path, you know how to use the appropriate dosage of suffering—just enough to cultivate a true understanding of love. Be certain, you have the capability to cultivate compassion for all living beings, resembling a bodhisattva.

> STRENGTH: I balance my attunement to the immeasur-able amounts of invisible energies, remain completely present, and maintain calm in an elevated state of univer-sal love.

> PITFALL: Lost in fantasy and delusion, paralyzed by hopelessness, escaping it all through mind-altering substances.

> MONEY MINDSET: My warmth and compassion are well balanced with exceptional business sense for attracting astounding wealth.

> BREAKTHROUGH QUESTIONS: Is there a current circum-stance where my imagination is getting the better part of me? If so, how can I recalibrate to see this situation for what it truly is? How can I use this sense of suffering to offer help? What is the best environment for me to rest and renew? How is my relationship with money affected by my heightened sensitivity?

> AFFIRMATION: I vow to serve the suffering by breathing in, breathing out, and sending love.

Reminder: Any one marking in the hands cannot define us. We are composed of many aspects and are continuously evolving in awareness. Having these markings doesn't mean you will go through all the upside *and* downside descriptions. You may have found yourself immersed in one side or the other at different periods in your life. To build your toolkit, keep a journal and clearly identify how and what you did to transition from the negative to the positive. Also track how the negative was triggered when you were in the positive.

My Money Map Exercise

Using the words in this book, describe the strengths and pitfalls linked to your Challenge Markings, if you find any, in either or both hands. Also note the associated Money Mindsets. (See the example on page 60.)

The Challenge Markings I See in My Hands

Right Hand

PAGE: _____ MARKING: _____

STRENGTH: _____

_____

PITFALL: _____

_____

MONEY MINDSET: _____

_____

_____

Left Hand

PAGE: _____ MARKING: _____

STRENGTH: _____

_____

PITFALL: _____

_____

MONEY MINDSET: _____

_____

_____

Note the markings you see in both hands on the blank
hand maps at the back of this book, pages 212–213.

Head Lines

How to Use Your Thinking System to Generate Revenue

> *"You have power over your mind—*
> *not outside events. Realize this, and*
> *you will find strength."*
> —*Marcus Aurelius*

THE HEAD LINE (Figure 35) in your hands represents the unique operation of your mental system. Nature has created a specific and decipherable track in the hand to depict how your unique computing system is programmed. How you plan, calculate, analyze, estimate and integrate ideas can be read from this major line in your hands. In short, the Head Line is examined to understand the thinking system of the owner.

The course of the Head Line reflects clear, steadfast, fuzzy or messy intellect as well as how much time a person spends thinking. Longer Head Lines indicate high requirements to apply intellectual capability. Short Head Lines belong to people who make quick decisions. No Head Line is better than another. Everyone comprehends information differently; people think and make decisions in different ways. Understanding your own method of decision-making and your mental attitude will help you in determining how best to apply it to generate revenue.

Included in this chapter are potential positions where the associated mental energy could be optimally used. These examples are provided with the Head Lines because the Head Line is a major line in the hand and is constantly engaged during money-making, spending, saving and strategizing activities.

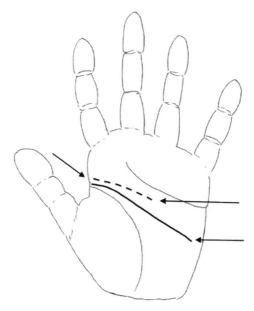

FIGURE 35: HEAD LINES, SHORT AND LONG

Following are markings involving some of the Head Line types found in the hands. Take note of what you learn in the following pages related to your Head Line types. I've selected only a few easy-to-spot examples. If you don't see your Head Line type, then move on to the next chapter. However, take a close look at your coworkers' or team members' hands to attempt to detect their Head Line design. You'll learn a lot about those who do have markings you see in this book. Be prepared to complete the My Money Map Exercise at the end of the chapter for yourself or even for someone else. Make this book work for you to plan for your financial freedom.

Bottom Line Mind

When a Head Line travels across the palm on a steady course, then flips upward at the end (Figure 36), its owner will have an uncontrollable urge to get the conversation to the bottom line. It's as if the pinkie finger, which conveys to quick mindedness, is invisibly pulling the end of the Head Line upward. Here we have someone who is highly alert, shrewd and clever.

The long Head Line implies a supercomputer, and the upward flip denotes the ability to dart to the bottom line at lightning speed. This person is aware of what is really going on behind the scenes. He or she is quite astute and can condense a two-hour movie into two sentences. The author of the CliffsNotes who summarized the literary work of *War and Peace* probably had the Bottom Line Mind Head Line configuration.

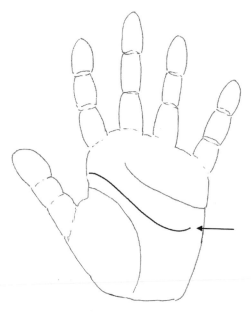

FIGURE 36: BOTTOM LINE MIND

One owner of this line configuration told me, "It can be very painful to listen to someone drag out a story or an explanation when I already know where it's going. I've learned how crucial it is to be patient and to bite my tongue so that others can finish speaking."

It's important for the person with this marking to find an approving audience for his or her agile, extra-aware, no-nonsense mind, otherwise he or she may be considered callous and ruthless. When someone is wired for getting to the bottom line and telling it like it is spontaneously, he can appear quite insensitive. Friends and family may not have praised his or her urge to "get to the point" or his or her skill in doing so. The best remedy is for such a person is to have an outlet in which he can be fully engaged in truth-telling, while being in an arena where he is accepted and acknowledged for that skill.

Potential positions include consultant, coach, heart surgeon, attorney, security officer, air traffic controller, emergency medical technician, fire captain, magazine, book or podcast editor, sports competitor.

STRENGTH: Count on me to get to the point without fluff.

PITFALL: Inconsiderate, alienate friends and family, self-condemnation.

MONEY MINDSET: I use my laser-sharp mind effectively in self-employment or in an occupation where I am highly appreciated and financially compensated.

BREAKTHROUGH QUESTIONS: What's my secret to tactfully get others to the bottom line? How would another few seconds of patience serve another person in conversation—and the team? What's the best way to inform others of my immense impulse to get to the point of the conversation *and* that I still care about them?

AFFIRMATION: With practiced patience and care, I am a success everywhere.

The Advocate

The Advocate has a Head Line originating inside and below the start of the Life Line, just above the inset of the thumb (Figure 37). This is the Mars Mount.

If you have this configuration, you're watchful and mentally alert. You can be headstrong about seeing both sides of the same coin. You're a determined debater, but you can seem argumentative to someone not interested in debate.

One nine-year-old child I read for had this marking. After I told him he was an Advocate, he told me he had recently been assigned to be a bully buster at school. The Advocate is designed to stand up for others who are unable to stand up for themselves. The Head Line, which represents the mental system, is dipping into the Mars Mount. Mars is a protector, capable of combat for his or her cause. The owner's mental processor (Head Line) is fed by the courage and bravery of Mars, the warrior.

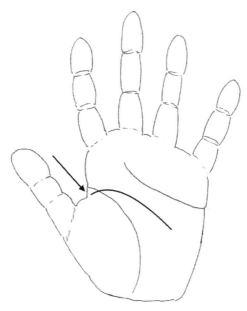

FIGURE 37: THE ADVOCATE

The advocate thrives when seeing things differently. Such a person makes an excellent social, political or environmental activist, waging war for the underdog.

That nine-year-old child I read for is now attending college, where he plans to study and advocate on behalf of the environment.

Potential positions include activist, campaigner, futurist, conservation scientist, urban planner, environmental engineer.

> STRENGTH: I am steadfast in considering contrary view-points and contribute many perspectives to uphold the conversation on behalf of the marginalized (persons, places or animals).

> PITFALL: Must be right and win the argument, quarrelsome.

> MONEY MINDSET: For the cause, I use my skills of assertive thinking in tactful, savvy ways; limitless riches stream to me.

BREAKTHROUGH QUESTIONS: In what ways and at what times in my life has activism presented a deep sense of triumph? How can I best use my advocacy skills where I am most disturbed? How can I best apply criticism to correct, improve and change without humiliating or embarrassing another person?

AFFIRMATION: My strategic action creates the life I want.

Only Solutions

If the Head Line starts with a curve coming down from the index finger, its owner is constantly on point to solve problems. Their motto is "Only Solutions." They are highly motivated to formulate action plans based on high ideals, vision and dreams. They are known best for their killer problem-solving skills

The line acts like an antenna, downloading inspiration, strategies and solutions to the leader within. The owner of such a Head Line is capable of brilliant influence through a continual flow of ideas for the betterment of the territory in which he or she resides. He or she

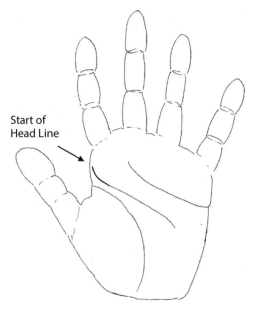

Start of
Head Line

FIGURE 38: ONLY SOLUTIONS

is highly motivated to respond to other people's ideas, problems and plans in the form of solutions.

Potential positions include troubleshooter, detective, mission control operator, respiratory therapy technician, repair person, emergency medical technician or paramedic, sports medicine physician, hydroelectric plant technician, forest firefighting and prevention supervisor, electrical power-line installer or repairer, industrial engineer.

> STRENGTH: I inspire and offer expedient solutions with a high level of confidence.

> PITFALL: Lacking emotional sensitivity when in solutions-only brain.

> MONEY MINDSET: I am on the road to riches with highly revered solutions.

> BREAKTHROUGH QUESTION: How could being more considerate of others' feelings and values help my solutions to be better received?

> AFFIRMATION: "Failure is not an option." —Gene Kranz, *Apollo XIII* mission control

The Octopus Brain

When the Head Line is clear and extends with consistent thickness straight across the hand, terminating one-quarter to one-half inch before the edge of the palm, you'll find the Octopus Brain.

This person won't feel fulfilled unless she has an avenue in which to use her multifaceted system of comprehension and analysis. Think of this very long Head Line acting like an eight-armed octopus that must be in full synthesis mode in order to feel a deep sense of satisfaction. Each of the eight arms is equipped with numerous sense-gathering suction cups, too.

Richard Unger named such a long, clear Head Line the Octopus Brain. I relay the sea creature analogy to my clients and watch their eyes open wide. In unison their body language matches their voice, saying, "That's me!"

This super-synthesizing Head Line has definite mental require-ments—large, important projects with massive amounts of data.

If you are the owner of an Octopus Brain Head Line, a sure sign that you're not using your full potential is relationship problems. By initiating problems in relationships with others, you give yourself juicy problems to wrestle with. This makes the octopus very happy, in a sea creature kind of way.

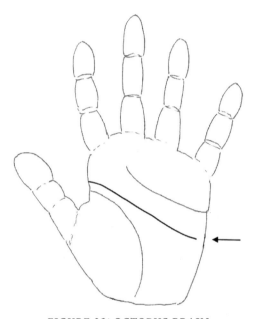

FIGURE 39: OCTOPUS BRAIN

Potential positions include long-term city planning, operations manager overseeing numerous sites, property manager, director of day-care centers, systems manager, business or data analysts, accountant, researcher, judge, criminologist.

> STRENGTH: I use my exceptional mental aptitude to fully engage in colossal complexity, successfully synthesizing large amounts of information.

> PITFALL: Unused octopus limbs, provoked problems to solve in relationships.

MONEY MINDSET: I am generously compensated as I exercise my ability to engage in the complex synthesis of information for the company or my own business.

BREAKTHROUGH QUESTION: When was a time that I felt most fulfilled managing large, important projects with massive amounts of data?

AFFIRMATION: "What the mind of man can conceive and believe, he can achieve." —Napoleon Hill

The Simian Line—Intensity

Sometimes the Head and Heart Lines are fused together into one channel (Figure 40). If you see one straight line crossing the entire hand and you can't see both a Head and a Heart Line, you've found a Simian Line.

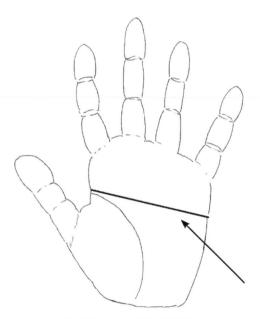

FIGURE 40: INTENSITY

This line acts as a divide separating the upper and the lower areas of the palm. The divide resembles a tightrope. Walking a tightrope takes extreme balance, penetrating focus, internal discipline, training, skill and courage. Now imagine walking on a high wire while it is being pulled in opposite directions, like the rope in a tug-of-war. Even more focus would be required to stay on the wire. That is the challenge facing people with Simian Lines. You may find yourself walking quickly, if not sprinting, back and forth between opposites. You may notice that others do not operate with the level of passion and intensity you have. Conversely, others may not understand why you are so concentrated on the task at hand. There is nothing wrong with you. You simply have tremendous ability and energy to focus. You are learning to harness and apply that power effectively.

If you wear this special line, you engage life at an extremely high level of intensity. In the positive, you approach projects, work and relationships with piercing focus. It's crucial for you to have a very important project to which to apply your concentrated mental and emotional self.

In the negative, you may feel challenged to communicate effectively; the thinking system (head) is tightly interwoven with your feelings system (heart), and therefore influences how the words flow out of your mouth. You may think you are being very clear with another person, but they just don't seem to get what you're saying. This causes you to feel misunderstood. Likewise, words coming to you from another person may become garbled or may be misinterpreted. This can be frustrating for both parties. Your job is to stick with it: keep articulating your thoughts as best as you can, with heart. You are on the path to communications mastery.

Allow yourself to act, react and retreat, and accept yourself in doing so. Although you think and feel deeply, you believe others don't sense that about you. As you "over-process" on the inside, others may see you as either a runaway freight train, or aloof and uncaring. Your job is to communicate in a variety of ways so that you will be understood. Practice, practice, practice!

Give yourself time to percolate those intense feeling-thoughts. Clarify your desires. To release interior tension, engage in physical activities such as running, racquetball, kayaking or yoga. As you embrace the unity of your heartfelt mental processing unit, you will be transported to new levels on your personal evolutionary journey.

High profile people with Simian Lines include Tony Robbins

(master coach/motivational speaker), Mel Gibson (director/actor), Anthony Hopkins (actor), Joaquin Phoenix (actor), Steven Tyler (singer/songwriter), Robert De Niro (actor), and Hillary Clinton (former U.S. presidential candidate).

> STRENGTHS: Excellence in communication results from my determination and persistence.

> PITFALL: Endless misunderstandings, retreat into a voiceless life.

> MONEY MINDSET: With intense drive I can be counted on to gracefully walk the tightrope, as a treasured asset to any team or organization, or as an entrepreneur.

> BREAKTHROUGH QUESTIONS: How could deeper interaction (communicating) with a business partner or colleague increase my (or our) revenue? What is the best avenue to receive feedback regarding my communication skills? Am I up to big-enough projects that keep me fulfilled?

> AFFIRMATION: "My poise is built upon a rock. I see clearly and act quickly." —Florence Scovel Shinn

My Money Map Exercise

Using the words in this book, describe the strengths and pitfalls linked to your Head Line types, if you find any, in either or both hands. Also note the associated Money Mindsets. (See the example on page 60.)

The Head Lines I See in My Hands

Right Hand

PAGE: _____ MARKING: _____

STRENGTH: _____

_____

PITFALL: _____

_____

MONEY MINDSET: _____

_____

_____

Left Hand

PAGE: _____ MARKING: _____

STRENGTH: _____

_____

PITFALL: _____

_____

MONEY MINDSET: _____

_____

_____

Note the markings you see in both hands on the blank hand maps at the back of this book, pages 212–213.

About the Fingers

Appreciate and Enliven Your Personal Expression

> *"For in the true nature of things, if we
> rightly consider, every green tree is far
> more glorious than if it were made of
> gold and silver."*
> —Martin Luther

THE CHARACTERISTICS of each of your fingers show an associated current of energy and how that energy manifests itself in your life. Understanding the fundamental meaning of the fingers can provide insight into traits you can use in your life and how you might best apply those traits at work, home or in relationships. In this section we'll focus on finger elements to aid your financial fulfillment.

Apart from any other characteristics of the hand, long fingers typically belong to people who are patient and have a love of detail. Short fingers indicate hastiness and reliance on instinct. People with chubby fingers indulge themselves in worldly pleasures, whereas skinny-fingered people are dreamy. Knots on the fingers at the knuckles make spaces for facts and figures to swirl around in, so large knots belong to people who are exacting and methodical. When the fingers are smooth along the sides, you'll find an intuitive person. Similarly, the length, width, depth and shape of the Colorado River provide clues as to how the force of that river flows through canyons and flatlands. Likewise, the crown of the tree, branches, bark, collar where the trunk meets the roots and straightness of the trunk offer evidences about the health of a tree. When you see an upright and healthy-looking finger, the force of that finger is strong and readily available for use in a person's life.

93

Each of the fingers is associated with a particular deity from ancient Roman mythology. The index finger is named for Jupiter; the middle finger is named for Saturn; the ring finger is named for Apollo; and the pinkie finger is named for Mercury. To better understand the meaning of each finger, we'll consider these gods and how their attributes are associated with each finger. You have four fingers, and you carry with you the energy of all of them. However, you can determine which energy type you access most, prefer to use, and even excel at by determining which is the dominant finger on each hand, as explained in this chapter.

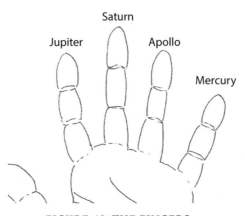

FIGURE 41: THE FINGERS

To begin, look at your right hand and compare the fingers to one another and identify your dominant finger. The dominant finger is the one that "looks the best." Just as you might look at four Sequoia trees in a grove and notice that one is most brilliant in color, stands most upright, with the healthiest bark, you can also identify your best finger. The dominant finger on your right hand indicates the Roman god whose character traits you display to the world—in public, in the office at work. The dominant finger on your left hand tells you which archetypal energy you access in private—at home. It's okay if on one hand you can't decide between two fingers. Choose both and blend the energies of both as you read them.

Steps for Reading the Fingers

1. Hold your hands with the palms facing you and the fingers held high.
2. Notice which fingers stand upright, and which ones are curved, bent or slightly twisted.
3. Identify the finger that captures your attention as best looking. This is your dominant finger.
4. See if you have a finger that appears especially weak. Weak digits are bent, crooked, leaning to the side, bent forward, or have a section that is shrunken or damaged in some way.
5. Make note of the finger(s) you see as most dominant.

If a finger stands out as weakest, you are less inclined to use the associated energy, or less comfortable in doing so. Learn more about this energy, and consider how you might embrace its associated qualities to support your personal expression. Understanding your weaknesses can contribute to self-improvement because it allows you to address them.

Besides the fingers, themselves, we'll also look at the middle sections of the fingers (Figure 42), because they represent activities in the material world. Money matters are primarily analyzed in the hands and fingers associated with the material world. The upper sections of the digits equate to the abstract and conceptual world—the world of ideas. The lower sections relate to the instinctual and physical world—the

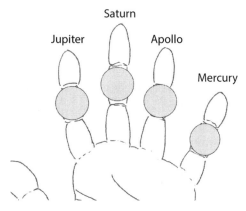

FIGURE 42: MIDDLE FINGER SECTIONS

world of body. With our focus in this book on prosperity and financial increase for use in the material world, you'll learn about the middle zones: Jupiter (index), Saturn (middle), Apollo (ring) and Mercury (pinkie).

Finger spacing must also be considered for money-making tips because the spacing presents clues to how open or closed a person is in particular settings. An inherently reluctant communicator most likely won't excel in sales. A Bohemian won't enjoy back-office postal work.

Take note of what you learn in the following pages related to your fingers, middle finger sections and finger spacing. Then be prepared to complete the My Money Map Exercise at the end of the chapter. Make this book work for you to create impactful money breakthroughs.

Jupiter—Visionary

In Palmese, your index finger is called Jupiter. Jupiter is the Roman god called the sky god. There was no god greater than Jupiter, after he overthrew his father, Saturn. He had grand visions, sometimes altruistic, sometimes selfish. His goal was to have a very large territory, with many loyal followers to carry forth his vision. Jupiter had lots of children, with the goal of maintaining and pursuing his high ideals. Central to his existence was to wield his power ambitiously in pursuit of high achievements. At the slightest sign of disloyalty, Jupiter pulled lightning bolts from his backpack and boldly cast them about, thrashing everyone and everything in their path. His intent was to demonstrate his power by pulling the trigger, but his ultimate goal was to unite and lead people toward his lofty and respect-worthy visions.

Consider all the ways you use your pointer finger in a day. You can bring it to your lips to quiet chatty cubical neighbors, point out directions to someone, beckon to a colleague, shake it at your dog, or tap it back toward yourself. There are lots of options to choose from. Achievement and inspiration out in the world motivate your pointer finger into action.

You'll find Jupitarian types leading teams as captains, directing people through disasters, soliciting contributions to charity, and influencing followers in worthwhile causes. It is important for someone with a strong, upright, index-taller-than-ring-finger to be in a position of influence and power, because this Jupiterian energy is a potent force for their success. Jupiterian activities include taking action on a lofty vision, activating choices to move people toward a common goal, sitting on a throne overseeing the kingdom or queendom.

If Jupiter is your strongest finger, you're at your best when you're in a position to stimulate positive change. You create a framework into which others may step forward. Claim your power, but do so appropriately. Your actions express your aspirations and priorities. While your ideals are strong and come from a revered source, you would be well advised to learn to wield your power with consideration for others. Disrespect for your ideas, vision and objectives can boil your blood. On a bad day, self-centeredness and pride can get in your way and derail your plans. Develop your skill at using the abilities of your followers. If you speak out harshly, apologize and clarify your intention to implement your vision.

If you work with a Jupitarian, gain insight into their dreams. Consider how you can support and even promote their values of higher-mindedness. Like Martin Luther King, who stood for the rights of all people, you might hear your Jupitarian say, "I have a dream." Mahatma Gandhi directed us to look inside and said, "A nation's culture resides in the hearts and soul of its people." The Dalai Lama points his index finger into the air, with his voice of inspiration for better living—aiming for a better world. On the other hand, disrespected Jupiterians can become egotistical, domineering and even dictatorial.

Jupiter key words include ambition, achievement, leadership, vision, power, high ideals, pride, preservation, territory, inspiration, benevolence.

STRENGTH: My vision fuels action into achievement.

PITFALL: Avoiding confrontation or overpowering others.

MONEY MINDSET: I am crystal clear and well-intended about my business and money goals.

BREAKTHROUGH QUESTIONS: With a millionaire mind what will I say "yes" to? What or who needs to be let go of to increase my fortune?

AFFIRMATION: "Leaders earn a heck of a lot more money than followers!" —T. Harv Eker

Looking at the palm of your hands, with fingers standing upright, let your eye glance around the twelve sections of the fingers. Notice if one zone stands out more than the others. Finding the dominant finger zone gets easier with practice. For now, see if you can detect your "best looking" finger zone, on either hand. The best section will be rectangular, not corseted, damaged or shrunken.

Middle Jupiter—Status

As previously mentioned, Jupiter represents ambition and confidence to achieve. When the middle zone of the Jupiter (index) finger (Figure 43) is most eye-catching of all twelve sections, the owner will place importance on practical elements related to Jupiter energy such as goals, priorities, competition and things. Things and status are symbols of quantifiable success.

The owner's shelves may be packed with trophies or their walls decorated with diplomas, certificates and awards. At their best they're keen on competition, keep their eyes on the prize and are honored to being measured. A bodybuilder, appraising the circumference of his or her bicep and the weight registering on the scale, is an example of someone with a strong middle Jupiter.

In the negative, they're focused only on the goal and appear to be extremely status-seeking to those less ambitious.

Beau and Jeff Bridges starred as brothers in a film where they played pianos at clubs. One brother was very pleased with, and motivated by, receiving "trophies" from each club. At the end of the film, when the two brothers had a falling out, the trophies were discovered to be shot glasses collected from the clubs where they had performed.

Another example is Jay Leno, with his collection of cars and motorcycles. At the time of writing this book, Internet sources report him having 286 vehicles (169 cars and 117 motorcycles). Leno doesn't hold a candle to the biggest car collector in the world—Sultan Hassanal Bolkiah, with more than 5,000 cars, which have a combined worth of $2.3 trillion.

If the middle section of your index finger is most eye-catching of all the twelve zones, then you'll be motivated by status and material gain. If this section is weakest—shrunken, cut or damaged—you'll detest your material goals being measured or judged.

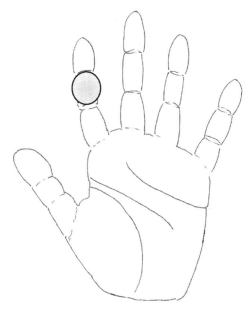

FIGURE 43: STATUS

STRENGTHS: I keep my eyes on the prize and am exceptionally motivated to get the goal.

PITFALL: Nothing else matters but status, feeling like a loser.

MONEY MINDSET: My planning skills lead to increasing promotions and accumulation of material reward. With doggedness, I break my glass money ceiling every year!

BREAKTHROUGH QUESTIONS: What is most important to me about achievement? Am I out of balance anywhere in life where having balance would increase my fulfillment even more?

AFFIRMATION: "My ships come in over a calm sea, under grace in perfect ways." —Florence Scovel Shinn

Saturn—Order, Money, Responsibility and Wisdom

In Palmese, your middle finger is called Saturn. In Roman mytholo-gy, Saturn (Cronus in Greek) is the god of time and harvest. As "old man time" he is the Great Teacher; you reap what you sow. His goal is perfection. Farmers aim for flawless crops. Business executives target the most effective use of time based on agreements and contracts. As a finger, Saturn is also considered the balance wheel. Notice how the middle finger divides the hand into two halves. The thumb side of the hand relates to action and results in the outer world. The pinkie side of the hand conveys considerations linked to the inner world (e.g., creative ideas)

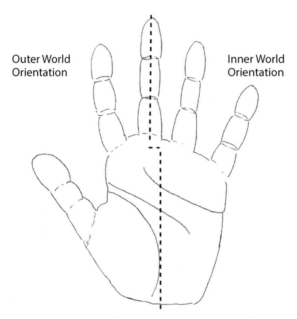

Outer World Orientation

Inner World Orientation

FIGURE 44: SATURN AS THE BALANCE WHEEL

You'll find Saturnians organizing their time, applying structure to organizations, and teaching people how to be responsible with their money, like Suze Orman. It is important for someone with a sturdy, upright, and straight Saturn finger to be in positions in which his or her skills for planning, investigation, discipline, correction and taking care of business are efficiently utilized. Value is a key word, so you'll find Saturnians tending to important tasks at home and work. The reason money is associated with Saturn is that money flows according to values. Saturnians save and spend money for things that have worth and importance to them. Saturn is the most practical of the four digits.

Saturnian activities include working to construct a better life by using time and resources efficiently; researching, clarifying and teaching people by following a system; harvesting growth after adequate time for development.

If your Saturn finger looks "good," you feel best when you are thrifty, industrious, dutiful and following rules based on your moral code. Organizing people, places and things, including words in an article you're writing, papers on your desk, shoes in your closet, food in your pantry or materials to teach, are all right up your methodical alley. On a bad day, when you're feeling out of balance, you can isolate yourself to process guilt, melancholia, bitterness or fear. Others may accuse you of being pessimistic, cynical, or doubting of yourself. Keep things in perspective, and avoid letting the seriousness of Saturn keep you down for too long. To climb out of the abyss, get a note pad and a pen and jot down what you appreciate about yourself, such as your ability to categorize, coordinate and discriminate. Include a few things you appreciate about others, too.

If you work with a Saturnian, give your workmate time to seriously discriminate, contemplate and organize. Like Benjamin Franklin, who said, "A penny saved is a penny earned," your coworker can offer a frugal game plan to the budget, project or business. You might hear your Saturnian say, "All good things come to those who wait," emphasizing the benefit of patience. Suze Orman promotes her "safety box" to keep your valuables protected from fire, flood and earthquake. Pilots don't approve the plane for departure until the multipage before-takeoff check list is in perfect compliance.

Rushing Saturnians will only cause them to dig in their heals even more deeply. Water their garden and witness, first hand, their astounding wisdom.

Saturn key words include responsibility, accountability, structure, value, organization, discipline, perfection, obsessiveness, patience, teaching, money and security.

STRENGTHS: Through diligence, my wisdom increases
with time, contemplation, patience and structure.

PITFALLS: Overly serious nature, pessimism, and fear about security.

MONEY MINDSET: I am generously compensated monetarily for implementing successful systems, following rules and abiding by policies, at the corporation or within my own business.

BREAKTHROUGH QUESTIONS: When life seems heavy and serious, what one new habit could I implement to lighten things up? How perfect do I need to be? How do I and others benefit from my higher wisdom teachings?

AFFIRMATION: "I am an irresistible magnet for all that belongs to me by Divine Right." —Florence Scovel Shinn

Good business is about the exchange of value and standing strong in our integrity. Honesty pays. The condition of the Saturn Line and the Saturn finger help you understand your strengths and weaknesses in creating a solid foundation and reliable structure for your work.

Middle Saturn—The Banker

Once again, looking at palms of your hands with fingers standing upright, let your eyes glance around the twelve sections of the fingers. Notice the condition of the middle sections of your Saturn (middle) fingers. Does either stand out more than the other eleven sections?

When this section is dominant, I read it as your inner banker, where you and money are a match made in heaven. Spending even the smallest amounts of money can cause stress. It's difficult for you to trust people with your money. Your strength is saving.

At best, the owner pays appropriate attention to money matters while also pursuing his or her purpose, without selling out to keep the savings account overflowing. If this zone is healthy-looking, the downside is focusing on security at the expense of fulfilling dreams.

Richard Unger, author of *LifePrints*, named this section "The Acorn Zone." One of many inferences of the middle finger is security. The middle sections of the fingers relate to the practical, everyday, material

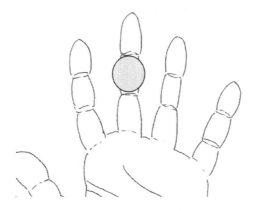

FIGURE 45: THE BANKER

world. If both the middle finger and this section of the finger look "the best," attention is primarily placed on material security. Storing acorns for a rainy day is a high priority for the owner with a dominant middle section on the middle finger.

Owners of an eye-catching Acorn Zone make excellent project managers, organizers and security agents. Self-preservation is a primary motivation for effort.

If this section is shrunken, cut or damaged, the owner will most likely experience money issues on a regular basis. He or she is prone to hoarding because of unresolved scarcity issues. Conversely, the owner may never save for a rainy day or struggle with the idea he or she can ever make money. I'd recommend studies and training with mindset and habit pattern development to gradually shift into new ways of seeing money and things of value. The owner would also be guided to look at other positive features designated in the hands.

If you find this section looking "good" on either of your hands you do well saving money, creating financial independence and are conscientious and financially responsible, unless other opposing variables in the hands challenge these attributes.

> STRENGTH: My frugal approach to life has resulted in a reliable nest egg for retirement while putting the kids through school and paying off the mortgage early.

PITFALL: Miserly, rigid and controlling when it comes to money and resources.

MONEY MINDSET: I balance my precious time, exacting energy and an endless supply of money with poise and joy.

BREAKTHROUGH QUESTIONS: What is frugality keeping me from doing or becoming? If nothing would diminish my savings for the next five years, how would I change the way I live?

AFFIRMATION: "It is man's divine right to have plenty more than enough." —Florence Scovel Shinn

Apollo—Individuality and Creativity

In Palmese, the ring finger is called Apollo. In Greek mythology, Apollo was the favored son of Zeus. He received appreciation, approval and applause from his parents, and was forever concerned with appearance. He was the shining performer, expressing his optimistic, brilliant, fun-loving and colorful nature. He was in the public eye as an artist and archer. As a master archer, he focused his aim on targets by developing his skills through patience and persistence.

You'll find Apollonians performing in the spotlight, perhaps dancing, singing, speaking or writing for an audience—but they must first overcome the fear of criticism. They thrive on a platform, expressing their most individualistic natures. Reputation and acknowledgment motivate their performances. So that he could be seen, the infant Apollo loved being to be elevated in his mother's backpack. The teen Apollonian loves being rewarded with approval and acceptance from parental figures and peers alike. Vanity, in the right amount, is a key ingredient for creating Apollo's best self.

Apollonian activities include being true to and extending your inner muse; uniquely expressing your ultimate craft in the spotlight; schmoozing and networking.

If you identify with Apollo and know you are called to claim the spotlight, persist! Identify your craft. Make it a priority. Identify impediments. If you are hiding, find ways to come out. Address your fears of a king-sized stage hook embarrassingly dragging you off stage. Reframe your fear of flying tomatoes into an opportunity to catch nutritious food. Don't let a fear of critics derail your compelling call to unique expression. There is a just-right audience who will rave for the creation you let flow through you. Vow that your mind, body and soul will shine brightly. Your magnetic flair is attractive. Integrate a passionate plan with discipline, and put yourself out there.

If you work with an Apollonian, support her craft by running lines for her upcoming play, admiring her fashion designs or encouraging her to splash her unique design on her canvas of choice. But know that she can become self-conscious and paralyzed by the fear of rejection.

Examples of living Apollonians claiming the spotlight are Lady Gaga, Beyonce, Snoop Dog, Billie Eilish, Taylor Swift, Vera Wang and Giorgio Armani. Deceased Apollonians include Marilyn Monroe, who lived in a number of foster homes as a child, and Ludwig van Beethoven, who was abused by his alcoholic father. These celebrities honored the call of the source of their individuality despite adversity in their lives. The sun can only shine for the artist when she is true to her essence.

STRENGTH: I am wholeheartedly open and willing to be true to my inner artist.

PITFALL: Hiding out, paralyzing fear of rejection.

MONEY MINDSET: Optimistically, I shine in my right light and magnetize a jackpot of money.

BREAKTHROUGH QUESTIONS: What one creative outlet stirs the most fear in me? What are three (or more) tools I can implement to transform anxiety and apprehension into courage and delight?

AFFIRMATION: "The Divine Plan of my life now takes shape in definite, concrete experiences leading to my heart's desire." —Florence Scovel Shin

Middle Apollo—Tangible Arts

When the middle section of either Apollo (ring) finger (Figure 46) is most eye-catching of the twelve finger sections, you'll find an artist who loves to design.

These artists employ their mental creativity for tangible master-pieces. Designer examples include: interior, graphic, clothing, jewel-ry, landscapes, faces and special effects. The list of designer options is endless. Operating a chic boutique, an elegant restaurant, a salon airbrushing fingernails, movie costume design, or even a stylish Zen

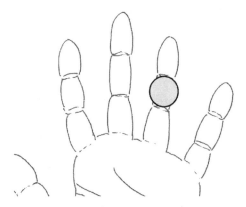

FIGURE 46: PRACTICAL ARTS

studio are passionate possibilities for the owner of a dominant middle ring finger. To dial into specifics, other areas of the hands would be consulted for strengths and preferences. For example, we might find a person with and Earth Hand shape, the Advocate Head Line and a dominant middle Apollo crafting combat knives or battleaxes.

In the positive, the owner has a healthy outlet for their passionate pursuit of beautifying the material world in a specialized fashion. In the negative, the owner would be lost in appearances and appear superficial.

Elton John is an example of a genius of applied artistry appearing on stage in wildly flamboyant costume. The lyrics in the song "Rocket Man" make me think he also has a Neptune Star, experiencer of the deep moods of the sea. (Read more about the Neptune Star on page 145.) Combining a strong middle section of the Apollo (ring) finger with a Neptune Star would portray an artist combining tangible beauty with his or her access to profound emotion.

STRENGTH: I style everything to be stunningly beautiful.

PITFALL: All show and no go.

MONEY MINDSET: As I allow my matchless muse to be revealed I am financially gladdened as a one-of-a-kind creative.

BREAKTHROUGH QUESTIONS: Am I creating in the area that truly calls to my heart? If not, what most deeply calls to my heart? When has my creative outlet been obstructed, and how? How have I been most successful breaking through creative blocks?

AFFIRMATION: "We all have a bank to draw upon, the Bank of Imagination" —Florence Scovel Shinn

Mercury—Messenger

In Palmese, the pinkie finger is called Mercury. In Roman mythology, Mercury is known as the messenger god. He has wings on his cap and on his sandals so that he can quickly transmit messages between mind and body. Mercury is a trader of information, products and people. He is analytical, brilliant, and eloquent learning faster than the speed of light. He is known to be precise, quick-witted and detached. He is swift in movement and agile in mind. He frequently travels between the sky, the earth, and the underworld. Mercury governs commerce and trading, public media and the worlds of diplomacy and persuasion. You'll find Mercury involved with anything related to the transmission of information.

You'll find Mercurians cleverly link their thoughts to words in an instant. Mercurian qualities belong to brilliant comedians such as Lucille Ball and Jim Carrey, and to witty news reporter Trever Noah, clever detective Sherlock Holmes or super-brain Albert Einstein. They thrive on having information to communicate, unless their wings are clipped and they're restricted in some way. On a bad day a Mercurian can withhold information, distort information through trickery, or become verbose. If pinned to a regimented system, a Mercurian can become unstable, impulsive, indecisive and overly critical.

Mercurian activities include reflecting, reasoning and communicating ideas; interpreting, translating and disseminating information; bartering, negotiating and trading.

If Mercury is your best finger, you'll tip your teacup with your pinkie in the air, eloquently pronouncing, "Please, tell me something I don't already know." As you're reading this, you're most likely ready to jump to your next adventure. Before you do, consider how your quick, sharp, clever language affects others positively and negatively. Are others able to keep up, or do you leave them in a cloud of bewilderment? Can you capitalize on your gift for communication and adapt to their level of awareness? Of course you can! You have instant access to words and the awareness that goes along with it. Watch to see when you withdraw in the face of emotional misunderstanding. You feel closest to your mate, children and co-workers when you're free to discuss, banter and joke. Use your expertise for rhetoric, whether in writing, editing, speaking, singing, sign language, negotiating deals, trading or any linguistic activity.

If you live with a Mercurian, don't take either his everlasting thirst for curiosity or his verbal retreats personally. Give him room for critical thinking, analysis and word-juggling. He needs space and time to negotiate and strategize. Remember, he can be quite humorous and full of wit in his own unique way. A Mercurian is constantly scheming how to manipulate language, thoughts and ideas. At his best he is skilled at knowing how to listen and speak appropriately for the environment he's in.

Mercury key words include quick, agile, clever, sharp, reflective, insightful, witty.

> STRENGTH: With quick wit I effectively bridge a variety of ideas, thoughts, words and activities.

> PITFALL: Trickery, withdrawal, humor or sarcasm to deflect from closeness.

> MONEY MINDSET: I use my natural communication skills and insights to structure deals and swiftly handle financial complexity.

BREAKTHROUGH QUESTION: How can I use my wittiness to successfully close my next best lucrative money-making outcome?

AFFIRMATION: "Every day I choose the right words, the right thoughts!" —Florence Scovel Shinn

Middle Mercury—The Negotiator

When the middle section of either pinkie finger is more eye-catching than any of the other eleven sections on the fingers, we have someone who is quick and clever with material world communications. The middle zone of the pinkie finger is naturally 20% to 25% shorter than any of the other zones, so account for that in your inspection.

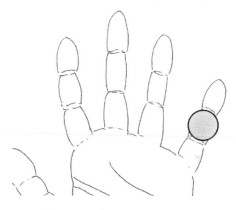

FIGURE 47: THE NEGOTIATOR

The owner has a keen sense of what does and doesn't work when it comes to business and negotiations. Jim Camp, author of the book *Start with No*, is a master negotiator. His training in the book offers a counterintuitive system for negotiating any kind of deal in any kind of situation—the purchase of a new home, a multimillion-dollar business deal or where to take the kids for dinner. He argues that a win–win approach is not the best way to make a deal.

Dealing with difficult situations allures the Negotiator's mental mastery into full command, and most likely, success. Search and rescue crews have designated individuals trained to incrementally deliver pertinent and accurate information about a family's loved one who has been lost in the mountains while hiking. The status of the body, when found, dead or alive, is delicately conveyed to the family.

When the middle section of the pinkie finger is especially small, damaged or cut, the owner's business sense will be challenged. I'd recommend they get help to negotiate buying a new car, house, building lease or anything where the price could be negotiated.

A person with a dominant middle pinkie section might do well as a translator, detective, strategist, broker, company merger, peace or hostage negotiator or mediator.

> STRENGTH: My brilliance dwells in my clever communications to negotiate for ideal outcomes.

> PITFALL: Strategizing when it's time to play, tricking people for the fun of it.

> MONEY MINDSET: I settle for nothing less than top dollar for access to my quick, sharp and clever strategizing expertise.

> BREAKTHROUGH QUESTIONS: How is withholding my mental dexterity impeding my income-generating ideas? If I were confident of my skill as an effective negotiator, what next step would I take on my path to financial freedom.

> AFFIRMATION: "I am awake to my good, I never miss a trick." —Florence Scovel Shinn

Finger Spacing

You've learned that the quality of each finger and the middle section of each finger contribute to analysis of one's strengths, weaknesses and preferences. Now we'll look at the meaning of space between the fingers. To gauge the spacing between the fingers, shake your hands then hold them comfortably up in the air, facing you directly. Compare people's hands to develop your eye for recognizing finger spacing.

Bohemian

When the fingers and the thumb are all widely spread apart with noticeable space between each, you'll find a Bohemian. These people are typically confident, independent, impulsive, liberal, open to new experiences—even wild, and usually unconcerned with social norms or what people think. There's a magnetic and radiant presence about them. A Bohemian child will take over the toy section at the thrift shop, naturally attracting and admitting others on her terms. Adults will be off the grid, traveling in a van across the country, showing up in unconventional ways. Conversely, the Bohemian might be running

FIGURE 48: BOHEMIAN

a maverick-like business, with liberal guidelines for work productivity. With wide open fingers, air and money have plenty of room to flow. Bohemians may be extravagant spenders and/or quite generous with donations. Owners need to take extra care when spending, if their plan is to become financially independent. A business niche would be helping others have what they have—freedom.

Tight

If all your fingers and thumb are held tightly together, you may be cautious, conservative and guarded. You're on the shy side, self-contained, contented with simplicity and consistency. You're probably a good saver, even penny-pinching when it comes to spending. Spending even the smallest amounts of money could cause anxiety for you. You most likely judge others for their money habits because you're disciplined and careful to live below your means.

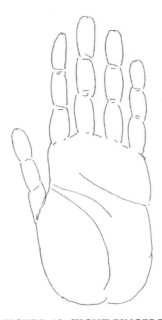

FIGURE 49: TIGHT FINGERS

Space Between Index and Middle

Index and Middle Separated

If these two digits are noticeably separated from one another you'll find someone who takes action when he or she is good and ready. In business, following systems will be a sore point. Tradition does not motivate action. Being in charge is the preferred option.

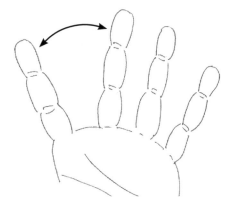

FIGURE 50: INDEX AND MIDDLE FINGERS SEPARATED

Index and Middle Tight

When these two digits naturally rest close together, you'll find someone who depends on others and authority. They like to know the rules before taking action. In business, he or she will require reviewing contracts and agreements before signing on the dotted line.

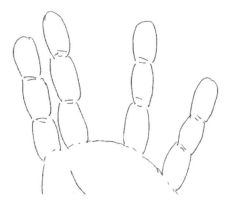

FIGURE 51: INDEX AND MIDDLE FINGERS TIGHT

Space Between Middle and Ring

Middle and Ring Separated

If your middle and ring fingers are spread apart, being in the spotlight is not important, and you're not easily influenced by popular opinion. You have an independent mind and a free spirit ripe for bending rules. Planning your financial future probably sounds unexciting and constrictive. New habits can be made, but saving money and conforming to the perceived money-making systems might be like scratching your nails on a chalkboard. If you dream of financial independence, but find the steps sound exhaustive and unappealing, get a coach or advisor, someone to help you become and stay accountable for reaching your money goals.

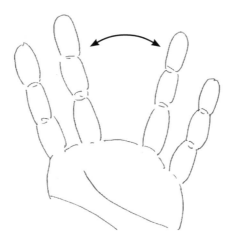

FIGURE 52: MIDDLE AND RING FINGERS SEPARATED

Middle and Ring Tight

If your middle and ring fingers are close together, you probably have concerns about material security and coming out into the world. You may be influenced by commonly accepted opinion. You are attached to outcomes where you'll have peace of mind which, for you, comes with security. Without considering the other elements in your hands, having a day job may best suit you, where you'll have a dependable and consistent source of income. Replace potential doom-and-gloom self-talk with exciting possibilities. You'd do well in jobs involving building and computer security, holding people accountable and project managing.

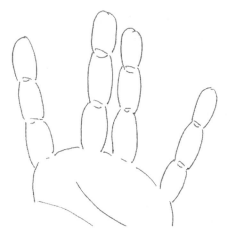

FIGURE 53: MIDDLE AND RING FINGERS TIGHT

Space Between Pinkie and Ring

Pinkie Separated from Ring

If your pinkie is splayed away from your ring finger, your ideas, opinions and thoughts are numerous and unaffected by popularity. You're an independent thinker. You need your space to contemplate and investigate. Because freedom is important to you, you need work or business life where you don't feel hemmed in. If the pinkie finger is

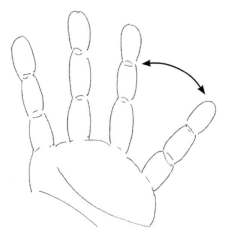

FIGURE 54: PINKIE AND MIDDLE FINGER SEPARATED

almost falling off the hand, you have an extreme sense of independence. Being alone comes easy to you and is desired. This is a sign that you could be dodging important conversations and that relationships at home and work could be suffering as a result. Find work to accommodate your preferred mode of operation and find ways to come out of isolation and interact with co-workers, employees or bosses at least 10% of the time.

Pinkie Tight to Ring

When the pinkie is held closely to the ring finger, we have someone whose ideas and speech are based on public opinion and accepted thought. Speaking out on their own behalf is difficult. What line of work would best suit this person's communication style? Actors and newscasters read scripts as they perform. Vocalists sing songs written by songwriters.

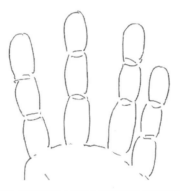

FIGURE 55: PINKIE AND MIDDLE FINGER TIGHT

My Money Map Exercise

Using the words in this book, describe the strengths and pitfalls linked to your fingers, middle section of fingers and finger spacing in either or both hands. Also note the associated Money Mindsets. (See the example on page 60.)

Eye-Catching Fingers and Traits I See in My Hands

Right Hand

PAGE: _____ MARKING: _____

STRENGTH: _____

_____

PITFALL: _____

_____

MONEY MINDSET: _____

_____

_____

Left Hand

PAGE: _____ MARKING: _____

STRENGTH: _____

_____

PITFALL: _____

_____

MONEY MINDSET: _____

_____

_____

*Note the markings you see in both hands on the blank
hand maps at the back of this book, pages 212–213.*

Gift Markings

Flagships for Financial Fulfillment

> *"Every adversity, every failure, every heartache carries with it the seed of an equal or greater benefit."*
> —*Napoleon Hill*

SPECIFIC LINE FORMATIONS create various gift markings (Figure 56). Not everyone has a gift marking. Some people have three or more. When people hear this expression, "Gift Marking" it sounds sexy and inviting. People want to have one and are eager for me to point it out and speak about its meaning. However, you'll learn here that these glyphs come with a distinct warning that must be grappled with for the genius to come to light.

Gift Markings identify precise talent that is so potent that they are a call to the owner of the hands for immediate attention and use. If the special talent is not used, there is an associated challenge. I want to help you see the associated challenge, like a flashing road sign, and give aid to your decision to pursue the mission of the marking.

The Gift Marking system I learned in 2004 from Alana Unger, wife of Richard Unger who formulated the system, has been one of the most remarkable parts of my hand-analysis journey. I've taught a 22-hour Gift Markings course where I've compiled extensive contents, handprint and photo examples and stories, and have taught it over the years since 2012. Besides witnessing the testimonials from my clients, long-term students and their clients have also substantiated my findings of the enormous power demonstrated by these tiny features in the hands. Pamelah Landers has also done extensive research and

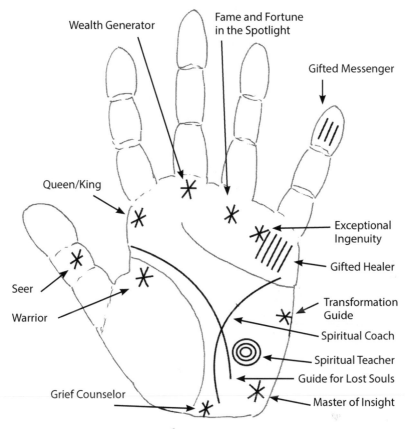

Wealth Generator

Fame and Fortune
in the Spotlight

Gifted Messenger

Queen/King

Exceptional
Ingenuity

Gifted Healer

Seer

Warrior

Transformation
Guide

Spiritual Coach

Spiritual Teacher

Guide for Lost Souls

Grief Counselor

Master of Insight

FIGURE 56: GIFT MARKINGS

practice with Gift Markings, and has authored insightful books on them. Search for her books online.

It's important to note that individuals do find reasons, whether consciously or unconsciously, not to inhabit their exceptional ability indicators. For example, someone may be a Gifted Messenger but getting that message clarified and distributed to the masses requires stillness to tune in and hear it—along with time management. A sure sign the message is blocked appears as one running but getting nowhere fast.

These distinctive etchings illustrate aptitude, ability, skill, capability, qualifications and high potential. But will they be realized? The more Gift Markings in the hands, the more loudly each will call to be noticed. But which ones need the most attention and consistent outlet for expression? One of my certification students who had several of these markings in her hands likened each one to a pack of wolves—some hungrier than others.

You will now learn about various Gift Markings, how to spot them in your hands, learn what to do to bring them to life and how to handle the attached challenges that are promised with each one. Because Gift Markings are so significant when spotted, I'm including potential career positions to consider for many of them.

Jupiter Star—The Queen or King

When you find a six-, seven- or eight-pointed asterisk on the mount of the pointer finger, or to the side of the mount, you'll find someone who must have an appropriate throne from which to wield his or her power in order to feel fulfilled.

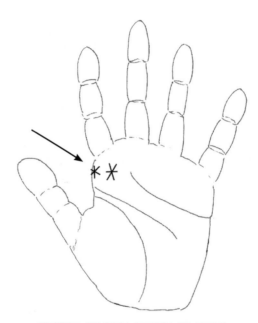

FIGURE 57: THE QUEEN OR KING

A star in this location offers a gift of high achievement like that of the valedictorian. The qualities of Jupiter must be at the centerpiece of their life for ultimate fulfillment. Jupiter is the Roman name. Zeus is the Greek name. As mentioned previously, he spent many years strategically planning how to overthrow his father, Saturn. He was successful. This reflects the energy in this glyph packed with drive, ambition, inspiration and motivation.

It's important for the owner of this star to employ the power and claim a queen- or kingdom that fits their visionary and strategic thinking. The super-achiever has a very long uncompletable, ever-expanding to-do list. They are driven to do way more than the average person and are likely to be overachievers. An unrelenting inside pressure pushes to get more done with an unrealistic schedule. Calendars of high achievers are filled up with all sorts of wonderful goals to triumph. Someone like myself may have three stars on the Jupiter Mount. A three-star array summons a leader of leaders.

For this individual, balance comes by getting real about the to-do list: make it realistic. It's common for the high achiever to feel frustrated with the sense of always being behind—there's more to do. Learning to delegate tasks that are not necessary to be done directly by the king or queen, so that he or she can focus on the royal choices, will help fulfill the "something bigger" that is calling.

On the path to greatness one will inevitably land in the valley of helplessness and overwhelm. The vision and the ideals are so big and expansive it is literally impossible for one person to accomplish all that he is being called to undertake. It's crucial to have a strategic list of priorities and skills for managing people. I've found women reluctant to step into this mighty role because they abhor confrontation. Leaders must confront. That's a fact. Therefore, I advise clients to look at confrontation differently. For example, get curious about the conflict. Ask questions. Don't defend or take disagreement personally.

On the downside, the owner of the Jupiter Star will play too small. He or she makes the boss look good or expresses power through a child, making sure the youth is in a power position.

Success in work, and financial reward, come through developing and implementing management skills. Being in charge of a group, overseeing a realm, can apply in many career scenarios.

> STRENGTH: I am unstoppable on this throne where I belong, managing people, expectations and conflict, strategically, for the highest good of all.

PITFALL: Leadership avoidance, excessive need for control, lost in the sea of helplessness.

MONEY MINDSET: I enjoy the financial rewards of super-achievement with the most fitting people in my empire where everyone thrives.

BREAKTHROUGH QUESTIONS: Am I aware of my leadership capabilities? Assuming so, what are they? *[Make a list.]* What do I do just for fun and how often? In which circumstances have people turned to me to wave my power scepter as a guide, way-shower or director? Do I have the "right" people in my king/queendom? If not, what will I do about it, and when? Am I helping someone else build their business, or building my own?

AFFIRMATION: My rightful throne expands as I pursue my vision, galvanizing change, with grace and ease.

Saturn Star—The Wealth Generator

The Saturn Star looks like a six- or eight-pointed asterisk etched onto the mount under the Saturn (middle) finger (Figure 58). The vertical line in the configuration consists of Saturn Line energy.

The Saturn Star indicates a horn of plenty. When the star twinkles on, shining brightly, the owner demonstrates uncanny ability for outstanding results for wealth. Miracles occur in their presence. What they touch turns to gold. It's as if they lay golden goose eggs, frequently.

At their best they know the appropriate use of value, and they bring their worth out into the world. They stand in the truth of their value, position themselves to spawn resources and help others create fortune. They're known to be wealth generators for others as well as themselves. I call this person a walking Wikipedia as a wealth of knowledge.

Most often, the owner must move through the challenge path before living life on the advanced path. The challenge path resembles the story of the cobbler who made shoes for all the children in the village but whose son went barefoot. They make fortunes for others but are unable to pay the rent because they question their own self-worth. The key is to stop spending all their time making money for other people or

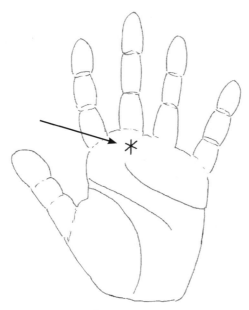

FIGURE 58: WEALTH GENERATOR

an organization and tune into what they love, nourish themselves and charge what they're worth.

Another example is a soccer coach having access to all the players parents' skills such as an electrician, contractor, chiropractor, veterinarian, nurse and more, when needed. A financial advisor putting people in touch with ideal ways of making money. An adoption counselor for animals, assuring good homes are found with delighted people.

If you own this star, acknowledge yourself as a resource hub, as the go-to girl, as a rich source of knowledge. Give to yourself first. What you have to offer is very important, you have "it" in endless supply and people need it. You are a perfect candidate for "coming into money."

The gift in this glyph is that the owner is learning to recognize his or her useful abilities and align him- or herself as a conduit for others' needs being met—all while receiving proper pay.

Look around and take an honest inventory of people who have benefited financially from your time, knowledge and commitment. Make a list of people, groups and organizations benefiting from your actions, ideas and counsel. Reassess your belief that "what they do is important, but what I do is so-so." With a slight shift in your mindset, permission to be selfish, you will manifest the abundance you're capable of creating.

Potential positions and organizations include financial advisor, computer technician, life or business coach, health care provider, director for nonprofits, adoption counselor for animals, Amazon (product distribution), Wikipedia.

> STRENGTH: My abilities to generate large amounts of money and resources is quite remarkable.

> PITFALL: Doubting or downplaying abilities.

> MONEY MINDSET: With grace and ease I stand in the truth of my value and produce generous payouts for everyone, including myself.

> BREAKTHROUGH QUESTIONS: How would I rate my self-worth on a scale from 1–10, 10 being highest? Am I charging enough for my services? Do I recognize my Midas touch—ability to manifest wealth and miracles? If so, how? What offerings do I have in my well of opportunities?

> AFFIRMATION: "Unexpected doors fly open, unexpected channels are free, and endless avalanches of abundance are poured out upon me, under grace in perfect ways." —Florence Scovel Shinn

Apollo Star—Fame and Fortune in the Spotlight

When the mount under the ring (Apollo) finger is impressed with a six-, eight- or more spoked asterisk (Figure 59), we have found an Apollo Star.

This person is poised for celebrity status trumpeting with exceptional creativity. In this case, "fame" comes as one allows their unique essence to shine through such that satisfaction, contentment and fulfillment are experienced. On the path to stardom the artist must grapple with the fear of rejection, apathy and hiding out. Serious crowd resistance will paralyze the talented individual until he or she finds techniques to work through the blocks. Finding the acceptable forum for their core creative expression is important. A tap dancer won't be received well in front of the audience expecting ballerinas.

If a star is stamped on your Mount of Apollo, focus your energies on keeping your artistic expression at the center of your life, allowing yourself to be truly seen. Find techniques to dissolve self-criticism and fear of disapproval from crowds and family. Keep the energy flowing by creating output such as designing clothing or jewelry, weaving tapestries, knitting hats, creating music videos or podcasts. Go for what your soul is calling you to bring forward from your deepest interior self.

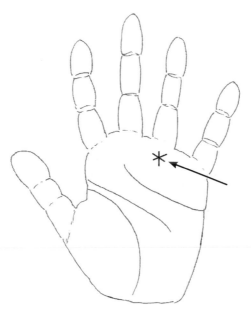

FIGURE 59: FAME AND FORTUNE IN THE SPOTLIGHT

Artist Georgia O'Keeffe is known for her colorful abstract paintings of flowers and bones. But her training was in a completely different style of painting. As she matured, she decided to let go of her training and paint the images in her mind's eye. She said, "I have things in my head that are not like what anyone has taught me—shapes and ideas so near to me, so natural to my way of being and thinking, that it hadn't occurred to me to put them down."

Potential positions would include any area where the owner would be wildly free to invent, design and create the majority of their working time.

STRENGTH: I follow the call of my deepest inner muse, giving it space and spotlight to shine fully and completely.

PITFALL: Invisibility, lethargy, paralyzing fear of rejection.

MONEY MINDSET: I invite and allow windfalls of wealth for the distinctiveness I bring forward, inspiring wholeness in myself and others.

BREAKTHROUGH QUESTIONS: Am I creating through writing and editing instead of my core love of cooking? Am I creating or will I create regardless of potential rejection and humiliation? Would I rather remain in hiding than risk rejection? If so, what is the cost? If I were receiving unlimited accolades in the spotlight, this is how I'd be showing up...

AFFIRMATION: "I spend money under direct inspiration wisely and fearlessly, knowing my supply is endless and immediate." —Florence Scovel Shinn

Mars Star—The Warrior

The Mars Star is a six- or more spoked asterisk located just below the start of the Life Line on the thumb side of the palm (Figure 60). The name Mars was assigned by the Romans. He's known as the God of War. The name Ares was assigned by the Greeks.

Ares was the least respected of the twelve Olympians by the Greeks because of his irrationality and battle frenzy. He had an uncontrolled lust for battle and bloodshed. Conversely, the Romans held Mars in high regard, second only to Jupiter (the sky god) in importance as the protector of the community. Mars' archetypal energy is active during battle for truth and justice.

People owning this star must have a cause: fighting for those who can't fight for themselves. Qualities include courage, risk-taking, bravery, daring and protective. Examples include Joan of Arc, Zena, Wonder Woman, Superman, Rambo, Judge Judy and Erin Brockovich. In everyday life, this energy fuels a mother who sticks up for her child being battered at school. One twelve-year-old girl with a Mars Star and three other classmates were victims of cyberbullying. The young girl confronted the bully, reported him to the principal, and he was arrested.

The challenge path for the owner of the Mars Star is rage, belligerence and/or cowardice and refraining from taking necessary risk. When someone identifies with the challenge path, my first question

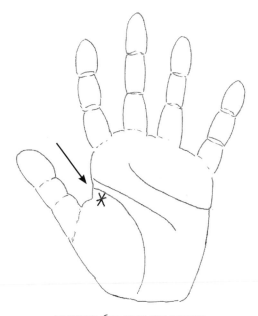

FIGURE 60: THE WARRIOR

is: What do you stand for, no matter what? What's worth fighting for more than anything? The answer will hint at their cause to fill the space of absent energy or dial back the excessive drive.

Famous Warriors include Mahatma Gandhi, an activist who employed nonviolent resistance and stood for peace and civil rights. Martin Luther King, Jr., is also known for his contributions to the American civil rights movement. He spoke of his dream of a United States that is void of segregation and racism. Arundhati Roy is an Indian author who is also a political activist involved in human rights and environmental causes.

Alicia Keys sings an inspiring song called "Underdog." Lyrics include:

So I sing a song for the hustlers trading at the bus stop
Single mothers waiting on a check to come
Young teachers, student doctors
Sons on the frontline knowing they don't get to run
This goes out to the underdog
Keep on keeping at what you love
You'll find that someday soon enough
You will rise up, rise up, yeah

Potential positions include activist, judge, police officer, Navy SEAL, military personnel, firefighter, whistleblower, CASA (Court Appointed Special Advocate for abused and neglected children) volunteer, halfway house supervisor.

> STRENGTH: I employ well-balanced strength, taking powerful action and risk for those who are unable to do so themselves.

> PITFALL: Righteous anger, belligerence, impulsiveness, spinelessness.

> MONEY MINDSET: I bring rich compensation to the causes I stand for, drawing upon the Warrior within.

> BREAKTHROUGH QUESTIONS: Do I choose appropriately between fight and flight? The healthiest outlet to use the immense amount of energy available to me is _____
> _____. *[Fill in the blank.]*

> AFFIRMATION: "I now transmute all enemies into friends, all inharmony into harmony, all injustice to justice." —Florence Scovel Shinn

Lines of Genius—Gifted Messenger

To locate the Lines of Genius, look at the upper section of the pinkie finger on both hands (Figure 61). There need to be at least three vertical lines on the upper section of the pinkie finger without having them on the upper section of the ring finger. If the upper section of the ring finger has three vertical lines and the pinkie finger has six vertical lines,

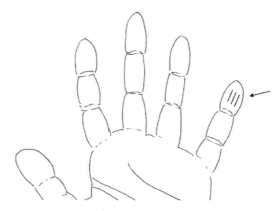

FIGURE 6I: GIFTED MESSENGER

then I would qualify the lines and call this person as a man or woman with a message.

The pinkie finger is called Mercury in Palmese. In mythology, Mercury wears wings on his hat and his sandals, giving the impression of flying between the world of concepts in the heavens, the material world of the Earth and the underworld of the psyche. Mercury (Roman) and Hermes (Greek) is known as the god of communication. Vertical lines are signs of yes energy.

The owner of this marking has a skill for brainstorming, communicating and, specifically, translating. He or she has the gift of explaining complex concepts to others so that they're simple to understand, and listeners "get it." For example, a choir director transforms the abstract language of music into something the audience can Understand. When a skier hits a tree at a ski resort and dies, the public-relations manager speaks to the media on behalf of both the victim who crashed into the tree as well as the ski business. The adage, "A picture tells the story of a thousand words" can be linked to the Lines of Genius. One client with this marking created a collage of images and won an award for conveying the importance of cultural diversity and non-judgment while in high school.

This glyph indicates a talent for decoding abstract concepts like hand analysis, metaphysics, science, higher consciousness and healing. The owner has a keen aptitude for translating nearly intangible matters into a language that can be quickly understood.

Shuffling papers on a messy desk, losing the mobile phone over and over again or feeling scattered are sure signs the genius is jammed. The man or woman with a message won't feel fulfilled if he or she is going nowhere fast. After assessing where my client is on the spectrum from full-throttle messaging to being lost in the translation, I offer exercises for development. These include:

Carve out time to write, speak, sing or sign.

Join a group such as toastmasters to practice.

Quiet down, discover your message and just do it!

I also ask the owner, "If you had a microphone and five seconds to deliver your most important message to a large audience, what would that message be?" A smile generally ensues because something came to mind. Some owners take their message for granted because to them it's so simple; yet to others it is complex.

Potential positions include orator, author, songwriter, screenwriter, singer, translator, sign language interpreter, workshop leader, scribe.

> STRENGTH: With tasks scheduled, I am wildly successful articulating my message—publicly.
>
> PITFALL: Hardworking on unrelated tasks.
>
> MONEY MINDSET: As a master messenger to the masses I magnetize money.
>
> BREAKTHROUGH QUESTIONS: Am I hiding in the audience instead of being at the podium? What is the message deep within me that is aching to come through? If I were to guess at the message within me, what would it be?"
>
> AFFIRMATION: "My endless good now comes to me in endless ways." —Florence Scovel Shinn

Gifted Healer

To find the sign of the Gifted Healer, look for four or more short vertical lines on the mount under the pinkie finger and above the Heart Line (Figure 62). The short vertical lines imply a flow of insights and awareness, provided the owner is allowing the stream as intended.

The owner of this configuration is being beckoned to heal—to help people piece themselves back together again. He or she acts as a growth catalyst by seeing the potential in another person when they are unable to do so themselves. Their words of inspiration and encouragement attune the person in their presence to go inward for answers, resulting in spontaneous growth.

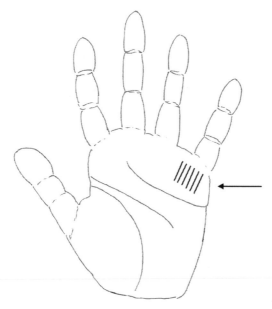

FIGURE 62: GIFTED HEALER

Medical stigmata has been assigned to this marking for over 100 years. Traditionally doctors and nurses had this marking back when they listened to the patient to gain insight into the cause of the ailment. In my eighteen years of reading hands, examples where I've seen it include: a wholistic doctor, photographer, esthetician, beautician, breast cancer survivor, ranger, longtime religious commune dweller, and a hike leader. Anyone in any position can wear the stripes; what's important is using the gift of growth consultant.

At her best, the owner is in touch with her own inner self. If she's terminally ill, she comes to terms with the illness. Perhaps the individual scribed with these stripes assists others through the shock, stabilization and transition through terminal illness, as a death doula would do. Vertical stripes are earned as the owner learns to listen and surrender to their inner guidance and deeper meaning.

The challenge is to live by trust, in their innermost messenger, whether he or she is going through their own healing crisis or managing healing crises surrounding them. Either way, he or she will face tough personal predicaments that could look like major illness or relationship issues. For example, the owner may be dealing with a child alcoholic, death of a child, mother in an iron lung for ten years, or fighting breast cancer herself for five or more years. Statistics, intellect and rational thinking are no way to navigate through such uncharted terrain.

Four lines indicates a knack for insight. Five lines shows someone who's probably active in some capacity as a healer. With six vertical stripes the owner must have a professional avenue for this portal to healing. It must be a major part of their life focus. It's not meant to be used occasionally. With eight or ten vertical lines they will be called forward as a healer to healers. Examples would include a head nurse, teacher for hospice workers or doulas, guide for emergency technicians or therapists to frontline firefighters. Individuals in these roles offer an ear and energetic space for the healer to return to wholeness after being defeated by their own or someone else's shattered life-puzzle.

On the challenge path, Gifted Healers find themselves in dead-end relationships that had no chance of working from the beginning. Or they may live inside brick walls in a life of isolation completely closed off to an intimate relationship. Or they marry late in life because Mom said, "If you don't marry now, you'll be too old and no one will ever want you." Another show-stopper is collecting broken-people projects and trying to fix them.

If you own this mark, listen for the summons to heal. What would it feel like to fully commit to a life receiving proper pay for work as a healer?

Potential positions include veterinarian, minister, therapist, counselor, coach, personal growth consultant, wellness practitioner.

> STRENGTH: As an intuitive guide I reveal sage wisdom, helping others live into their wholeness.

> PITFALL: Part-time unpaid healer, withholding truth to partner and self, trust issues.

MONEY MINDSET: My psychological and spiritual insights are highly valuable and I charge what I'm worth (and get it), facilitating astounding results.

BREAKTHROUGH QUESTIONS: Have I proclaimed myself to be and taken action for a life course as a healer? In what ways am I most successful at trusting and surrendering to what is true for *me?*

AFFIRMATION: "As an intuitive person I am never undecided; I am given leads and hunches, and go boldly ahead, knowing I'm on the magic path." —Florence Scovel Shinn

Seer Star

When a six-pointed asterisk appears in the middle section of the inside area of the thumb (Figure 63), you find someone with exceptional inner-eye wisdom. They bridge the rational, logical mind and the intuitive mind.

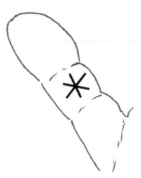

FIGURE 63: SEER

This section of the thumb is associated with the third eye of the chakra system. Chakras are invisible spinning wheels of light energy. They are non-material and etheric. Things happen first in the etheric realm, before coming into the physical realm. With a little detachment from material world judgements and demands, the owner of this star has the potential to just know. He or she uses the wisdom of his or her knowing to navigate through decision-making. Reason, analysis and spreadsheets are not required. At his or her best, the inner knowing is trusted 100%.

Examples include someone who sees when something is going to happen in the near or far future, like a car accident or an earthquake. Or they have a solid awareness of what is going on for a person, like a girlfriend being pregnant before the girlfriend even knows. An image or insight occurs in the mind's eye. Some owners call it a "flash," an "impression" or a "hit."

However, on the path to Seer mastery the owner will most likely withhold information for a variety of reasons. Reasons told to me include lack of trust in the vision, fear of ridicule if speaking about it, afraid of their own power to see, hands were cut off or buried alive in a past life for sharing or witches were burned at the stake. In some cases, the owners don't see what is obvious, such as health problems that need attention. He or she may not recognize being taken advantage of or mistreated. He or she can be blind to what is happening in their own life. They just don't want to see.

The owner of the Seer glyph understands the underlying connection between all things. It has been described as if everything is part of a unified field or universal grid where the tiniest occurrence has a profound and extensive wide-range effect.

Potential positions include aura reader, psychic, homeopathy practitioner, minister, meditation teacher, spiritual teacher, shaman.

> STRENGTH: I agree to bring clarity and action to my revelations.

> PITFALL: Not trusting perceptions, uncertainty, withholding visions, judging others as being wrong.

> MONEY MINDSET: I am well rewarded as a gifted seer, sharing my spiritual wisdom in a receiving atmosphere.

> BREAKTHROUGH QUESTIONS: If I had an internal crystal ball, what would I see? How might I benefit if I set reasoning aside, and just allowed what needs to come forward to come forward and out to the world?

AFFIRMATION: "Happy surprises come to me each
day. I look with wonder at that which is before
me." —Florence Scovel Shinn

Pluto Star—Transformation Guide

The Pluto Star is a tiny six-pointed asterisk on the outer edge of the
palm under the start of the Heart Line (Figure 64). It can also be located around the edge of the side of the palm in this area. A magnifying
glass will help locate a potential Pluto Star.

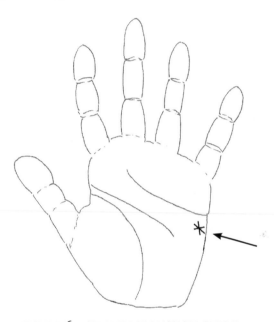

FIGURE 64: TRANSFORMATION GUIDE

The owner of this gift marking can provide a positive perspective
to a person who has experienced difficult change, once the owner has
worked through the associated challenge path.

One example of a drastic change occurred when Christopher
Reeve, age forty-two, was thrown from his horse, leaving him paralyzed from the neck down and wheelchair bound. Reeve is best known
for starring as Clark Kent in *Superman*. After the 1995 accident, with
the support of his wife, Dana, Reeve continued to live boldly and
started a foundation crusading for spinal cord injuries. The founda-

tion continues today, long after they both passed more than a decade ago.

People with a Pluto Star Gift Marking are roused forward with the courage to guide and transform people, groups and organizations to restructure their lives. This marking points to an individual who is deeply introspective into perceptions around death and rebirth.

The upside for the owner of this Gift Marking is the ability to be a change agent for good, through upheaval and devastating circumstances. A downside, however, can be that the owner becomes stuck in the undesired change and may feel like a victim.

When I meet with clients who are stuck, they often express loneliness. I ask, "Is there something to let go of that is keeping you stuck?" The answer might include a thought, a belief, a memory or perhaps letting go of assets related to grief.

Transformation Guides can turn the negative into positive possibilities, like Christopher Reeve (he most likely had the Pluto Star!). Those who do not have the Pluto Star marking can still be a Transformation Guide, though upheaval experiences may be less intense.

Potential positions include career coach for people whose careers end abruptly, narcotic or Alcoholics Anonymous sponsor, crisis volunteer, funeral home consultant, guide to former gang members, parole officer, safe house counselor, mediator, mortuary cosmetologist.

> STRENGTH: I am an expert at restructuring, transition, death and rebirth.

> PITFALL: Lost in loneliness, victimization, recklessness, forceful coercion.

> MONEY MINDSET: I am richly rewarded for my gift of introspection, seeing what needs to be destroyed in order to create room for what needs to be born.

> BREAKTHROUGH QUESTIONS: Are secrets destroying me that if released or revealed I'd find healing? How have the most difficult changes in my life best served me, and others? How can I help people or organizations face their demons and start new lives? Where is an ideal organization where my talents would be highly valued?

AFFIRMATION: "I am deluged with the happiness that was planned for me in the Beginning." —Florence Scovel Shinn

Line of Clairvoyance—Spiritual Coach

A Mercury Line that arcs around the lower, outer edge of the palm, known as the Moon or Luna Mount, shows the gift of deep insight.

People with Mercury Lines that curve like this are highly intuitive. They have exceptional talent to attune to and understand messages about the meaning of life. At their best, they claim this ability and use the gift of constant contact with "that which knows" as a spiritual coach or guide. This skill isn't something they necessarily learn; it's an automatic response system, like a dog hearing a dog whistle. The owner can't turn it on or off—it's automatic, and other people can't hear what the owner hears. Hearing can be interpreted as sensing an impression, seeing a vision, getting a block of downloaded information or in a variety of other ways. The key is the Spiritual Coach is constantly plugged into the source of existence. Their lives revolve around deciphering meaning in everything around them, such as a cloud formation in the

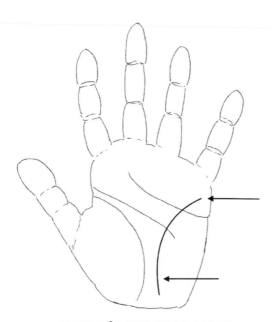

FIGURE 65: SPIRITUAL COACH

sky, a particular book falling off the shelf, a butterfly soaring in a continuous configuration or an intuitive hit. One woman with this Mercury
Line configuration told me, "Why do we need these human voices to
communicate?" implying her clairvoyant abilities.

At their worst, they doubt or fear their abilities and become alien-
ated from themselves and their core identities. (The core identity is the
deepest part of the self, and awareness of that self.) If the arc around
the Moon Mount falls on an Air Hand shape (see the later chapter on
Hand Shapes), or if the Head Line is long and straight like the Octopus Brain (see previous chapter about Head Lines), then the individual
may rely more on analysis, reason and rationality than their reliable
inner attunement system. Or he or she may feel like the kooky one, not
belonging, feeling left out. This can lead to depression. In her book *The
Power of the Spoken Word*, Florence Scovel Shinn said, "Prayer is you
telephoning to God. Intuition is God telephoning to you." She adds
"Many people have a busy wire when God telephones and they don't
get the message. Your wire is 'busy' when you are discouraged, angry
or resentful. Your negative emotions drown out the voice of intuition."

It's not uncommon for people with this curving line to experience
crises of meaning, because they have a deep longing to know the answers to life's big questions, such as "Why am I here?" and "What is
my purpose?" At some point, the material world comes into view as an
illusion and the real, inner world appears. When this happens, it is a
sign the "meanings expert" has been activated.

The best attributes of a Mercury Line come through when the
Mercury finger is straight. If the pinkie finger is bowed, twisted, or
damaged, then the current running through the line in the palm will
be impeded, making it more difficult to access inner awareness. Fingers
can straighten up with time, but this requires determination for honest,
conscious, communications on a continuous basis, with others and,
most importantly, with one's self.

Potential positions include spiritual advisor, child grief counselor,
lucid dreams coach, crisis of meaning consultant, transformation coach,
hypnotherapist, clairvoyant, intuitive.

STRENGTH: I understand messages from the universe
and offer my expertise as a meanings expert.

PITFALL: Alienation, stagnation, lacking trust, choosing reason over instincts.

MONEY MINDSET: My business of intuiting leads me to a bounty of fortune.

BREAKTHROUGH QUESTIONS: If I've lost hope, what is the best course of action for me now? How have I used crises of meaning to help others? Am I ready to advance to the next level as a life teacher?

AFFIRMATION: "I now give Infinite Intelligence the right-of-way." —Florence Scovel Shinn

Whorl in Moon—Spiritual Teacher

Whorls are commonly seen in fingerprints. However, when one unusually appears in either or both lower and outer area (Moon) of the palm (Figure 66), you've found a deeply introspective individual. The Moon Whorl isn't technically a Gift Marking, according to Richard Unger's system; however, having one indicates extraordinary potential. As with the other Gift Markings, positive and negative possibilities apply.

One definition I use, but not the only one, is Spiritual Teacher. I leave the ultimate definition of spiritual to the client because of the vast background of experience and preferred studies they have pursued. In a nutshell, to me spiritual is about awakening the spirit within the human. It's there all the time, but humans tend to armor up with blocks to their most authentic selves. The Spiritual Teacher will help guide people into the core of who they are at the deepest and most profound level. The effects of encounters with the teacher come through even while doing mundane day-to-day activities like doing the dishes or preparing a meal.

In hand analysis whorls relate to the element of air. Information swirls through the air from transmitter to receiver. Information and teachings are delivered through the air. The moon is related to our dreams, subconscious, desires to know the meaning of life. When you blend the whorl with the moon, we have a insightful teacher. Unlike other markings in the hand, this imprint is present at birth, just like the fingerprints.

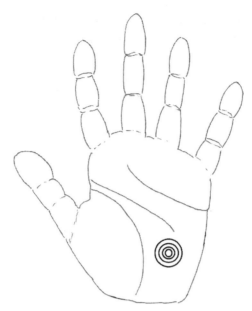

FIGURE 66: SPIRITUAL TEACHER

The Dalai Lama is considered a spiritual teacher. I don't know if he has a whorl in the Moon Mount of his palm, but he had this to say, "The more we pursue material improvement, ignoring the contentment that comes of inner growth, the faster ethical values will disappear from our communities. Then we will all experience unhappiness in the long run, for when there is no place for justice and honesty in people's hearts, the weak are the first to suffer. And the resentments resulting from such inequity ultimately affect everyone adversely."

Spirituality touches every aspect of our individual and collective lives. One who lives a spiritual life strives to, and is often able to, see into the true nature of reality where everything is connected. Nothing is separate. The Spiritual Teacher exemplifies this.

You don't need a whorl in your moon zone to do this type of work. Anyone who chooses can guide individuals into their interior world to realize their wholeness. At their best, the owner of this marking in this location is "called" to perceive meaning in everything. They inherently get impressions, insights or hunches that support the emotional, spiritual or mental needs of the individual in front of them. At their worst, they disconnect from their inner world and withdraw into isolation. Without effective tools, they can disengage from their gift when rejected or ostracized for their special abilities.

Potential positions include hand reader, counselor, life coach, teacher of the healing arts, meditation guide, musician, artist, motivational speaker, minister/pastor/chaplain/rabbi, medicine man/woman.

STRENGTH: The universe is the message board for meaning, and I understand.

PITFALL: Dissolution, stuck in the void, excessive fantasizing.

MONEY MINDSET: The magic money purse I imagine in my mind manifests triple-fold in my life.

BREAKTHROUGH QUESTIONS: Finish these sentences:
I have felt most contented as a spiritual teacher when I…
The avenues in which I prefer to apply my knowledge of higher awareness are…
If all fear of disapproval disappeared, I would follow my "calling" by…

AFFIRMATION: "I have a wonderful work, in a wonderful way, I give wonderful service, for wonderful pay!" —Florence Scovel Shinn

Moon Star—Master of Insight

When a star resembling a six-pointed asterisk appears in the lower, outer area (Moon Mount) of the palm (Figure 67), the owner has the capability of being a Master of Insight. In readings they most often acknowledge having sudden bursts of insights. This can happen randomly, such as during a conversation with someone, in a dream or while shopping at the grocery store. No specific setting is required.

The Moon Whorl in the palm is considered a dermatoglyphic and does not change. However, a Star in the Moon, as well as the other Gift Markings, can appear and disappear depending on what's happening in the owner's life. Stars in the palm are read more from a personality perspective because they are changeable. A Whorl in the Moon, or any other location in the palm, reflects the soul consciousness: what a person came here to do, as in a life mission.

On the advanced path, the Master of Insight trusts her sudden flash of intuition. She surrenders to her inklings and follows her "knowing." Owners have professed having "accidental brilliance." Alexander Fleming failed to tidy up his lab properly before heading off on vacation, and on his return found our first antibiotic—penicillin. On the challenge path the owner doesn't trust the hits they're getting and they can be found hanging out with the bozos! (A borrowed phrase from Richard Unger).

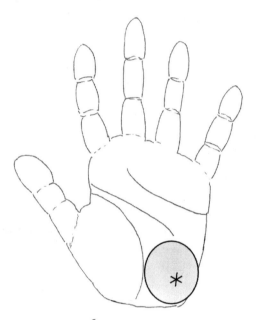

FIGURE 67: MASTER OF INSIGHT

I instruct my clients with this symbol scribed in their palm, "When you don't think you know, guess." Or, "When you have a problem to solve and you don't have a clue, turn to your mind palace, like Sherlock Holmes would do."

A Moon Star on anyone's hand indicates advanced spontaneous awareness, regardless of the position they hold. However, I went ahead and listed some potential positions for people who choose to focus entirely on this gift. These potential positions will also apply if someone has any other marking in the Moon—for example, Spiritual Coach,

Spiritual Teacher or a Head Line diving into the Moon (see Guide for Lost Souls, the next marking).

Potential positions include past lives therapist, Akashic record reader, inventor, psychic, metaphysician, ancient wisdom student, dream analyst, detective.

STRENGTH: I'm wicked accurate with my insights.

PITFALL: Cluelessness, alienation, ignoring intuitive hits.

MONEY MINDSET: I am lavishly compensated for the accidental discoveries that magically come my way.

BREAKTHROUGH QUESTIONS: When I track and trust my hunches, I realize… *[Make a list.]*
   I notice my hunches to be right on, especially when I'm in *[this]* state of mind *[e.g., quiet, dancing, meditating, golfing, etc.]*

AFFIRMATION: "I see clearly before me the open road of fulfillment." —Florence Scovel Shinn

Guide for Lost Souls

The shape of the Head Line reveals the nature of a person's mind. Straight Head Lines belong to people who are logical, rational, and practical thinkers. Downward curving Head Lines belong to individuals who are creative and reflective, with imaginative flair. If the line curves deeply into the lower part of the palm (see solid and dotted line options in Figure 68), you'll find someone with a natural capacity for diving into deep emotional waters with compassion, sensitivity, and even sadness.

People with Head Lines resembling Figure 68 consider ideas, thoughts and activities that are influenced by profound meaning in life. Behaviors associated with this Head Line style are likened to the mythological archetype Persephone. Owners of this line carving often feel the "snare" that Persephone felt after Hades kidnapped her to make her his wife. Held against her will, Persephone was trapped in the dark, dismal, gloomy underworld. If you have this deeply curving Head Line, you most likely understand the feeling of depression. It doesn't mean

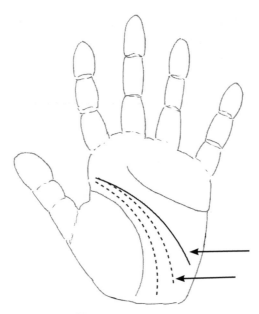

FIGURE 68: GUIDE FOR LOST SOULS

you are depressed, but you know what it means to be depressed. Like Persephone, you have experienced despair associated with "your life not being your own." You are sensitive and responsive to your environment, including the feelings of all beings. As Persephone matured, she opened her heart to Hades *and* to the other lost souls ensnared in the underworld. Likewise, as you mature you develop a deep compassion for others that can advance into life work as a guide for people who have been led astray or trapped. A deeply curving Head Line represents a potential path to mature into the Queen of the Underworld, handling hidden and all-consuming emotion, where reason has no place. Persephone also knew that she would return to the bright world above in spring each year. You have a genius for understanding others who enter into their own world of deep and unpredictable waters.

As the mythological story goes, there was a time when Persephone thought there was no way out of the underworld. Eventually, she did resurface out of the darkness, after choosing to do so, and realized her power in the decision and in her evolving journey.

Potential positions include counselor for physical, emotional or substance abuse, nurse, physician assistant, minister, teacher of students with severe disabilities, animal rescue/shelter, crying coach.

STRENGTH: I am able to be fully and completely present with deep sadness, maintain compassion, and steer others to their inner light.

PITFALL: Immobility, hopelessness.

MONEY MINDSET: I am richly rewarded for my willingness to remain open to deep emotion and my availability to other lost souls ready to "come back to life" again, feeling joy.

BREAKTHROUGH QUESTIONS: How have despair and grief best served me? How have I overcome feelings of powerlessness related to being a victim? What triggered my own resurrection and revival?

AFFIRMATION: "To the well-organized mind, death is but the next great adventure." —J.K. Rowling

Neptune Star—Grief Counselor

To locate the Neptune Star, the marking of the Grief Counselor, look to the bottom center of the palm bordering the wrist on both hands (Figure 69). They are very tiny, so you'll most likely need a magnifying glass. One, two or more can sometimes be found here. Only one star in this location is needed to qualify as a the Grief Counselor.

In Roman mythology, Neptune is considered the god of the deep sea. This depth of water symbolizes turbulent, unpredictable emotion. The gift indicates a knack for awareness as one flows through the natural cycles of tides and seasons. In the positive, the owner of this glyph

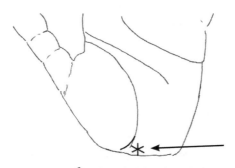

FIGURE 69: GRIEF COUNSELOR

is in a role holding space for others to traverse unimaginable depths of darkness, such as a mother losing her child in a car accident, now in depression, or a woman waiting for a heart transplant whose husband dies suddenly. The owner is directly in touch with his or her instincts and feelings. In the negative, the owner gets stuck in the well of human sadness. This can look like waves of intense feelings, sadness, delusions and even rage. In the worst case, this state of rage or sadness can last decades.

A person with this marking has the capacity to be with and explore deep, unfathomable feelings. One client told me, "I feel the collective suffering. I'm tapped into the dis-ease and it's heart-wrenching—and this gave me insight into why I am here and the work I have been assigned to do." A student with this marking said, "I experience over-whelming dark emotions, and after I move through them, I am able to hold the unholdable for others." With this marking it's important not to use logic and decision-making to either avoid the feelings or as a means to move through them.

Zürich, Switzerland–born Elisabeth Kübler-Ross (1926–2004) exemplifies someone owning a Neptune Star. According to a biography, she served as a volunteer during World War II, caring for refugees in various hospitals. After the war, Kübler-Ross volunteered to help in numerous war-torn communities. During a visit to the Majdanek concentration camp in Poland, she was deeply moved by images of hundreds of butterflies carved into some of the walls by people facing death. This profoundly influenced her thinking about the end of life. She had been disturbed by the treatment of the dying throughout her time in the United States and found nothing in the medical school curriculum at the time that addressed death and dying. She published her groundbreaking book, *On Death and Dying*, in 1969. The book outlines her theory of the five stages that dying patients experience: denial, anger, bargaining, depression and acceptance.

Here's a quote I read but don't know who wrote it: "Grief never ends, but it changes. It's a passage, not a place to stay. Grief is not a sign of weakness, nor a lack of faith… It is the price of love." The author has integrated loss into his or her life.

Potential positions include end-of-life doula, hospice worker, body donation consultant, poet, musician, medium, A.A. sponsor, deep sea diver.

STRENGTH: I go with the flow, riding the waves of intense feelings that well up inside and around me.

PITFALL: Taken over by and hostage to feelings, overwhelmed by life, rage, prolonged grief.

MONEY MINDSET: I am gifted in ways that facilitate transformation and triumph for both myself and others.

BREAKTHROUGH QUESTIONS: On a scale from 1–10, 10 being most, how open am I to my own deep inner well of emotions? How does giving myself the appropriate amount of time to explore my deepest feelings serve me and others? In what capacity am I using my talents and skills for awareness through the tides?

AFFIRMATION: "Love is really the only thing we can possess, keep with us, and take with us." —Elisabeth Kübler-Ross

Mercury Star—Exceptional Ingenuity

When an asterisk with six spokes is found on the mount under the pinkie finger (Figure 70), you find someone with exceptional mental qualities. This glyph is usually tiny, and you may need a magnifying glass to locate it. The star brings a sparkle, a lighting up, of the ingenuity and cleverness available for use by the owner.

By nature, Mercury is quick, sharp and clever. This is a person who has smart ideas, brilliant concepts and stellar strategies. Their mental dexterity is almost startling. It's natural to consider things from three different angles during problem-solving gyrations. It's crucial to have an outlet for his or her originality in thought and word. This person is inventive and highly resourceful and ideally uses cleverness to help themselves and others. Having a mechanism for feedback to validate his or her inventive ideas is important for bringing their Einstein-like genius to the light of day. A method for feedback could include a think-tank or having a Sherlock-type mentor.

The challenge side of this archetypal energy is reflected when the metaphorical wings are clipped. He or she will find it difficult to message effectively and instead highlight the crafty, cunning, quieter

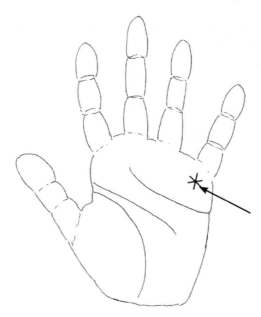

FIGURE 70 EXCEPTIONAL INGENUITY

side of Mercury. Or they may even be clueless about what's going on around them.

The film *The Social Network* depicts the startup of Facebook. Jesse Eisenberg stars as founder Mark Zuckerberg, illustrating a perfect example of exceptional inventiveness. He's a fast-talker, extremely quick on his feet, with tremendous mental clarity. His ideas come faster than people can grasp or respond to. He is, however, socially awkward and clueless about relationships, illustrated by the loss of his best and only girlfriend, who dumps him in the opening scene. If you recall, Mark Zuckerberg created the largest social network on the planet in 2004. He made his genius functional.

Another example of Mercury in flight: Artificial intelligence (AI) researchers and developers creating programs *to learn* from users and vast amounts of data so questions to Siri and Alexa can be quickly answered.

In an article by Michael Lagapa called "How Siri Works: Voice Recognition on a SmartPhone," he writes, "With the variations and subtle nuances we have in our speech there are an infinite number of ways to construct sentences. Mimicking the complex way humans comprehend speech into a programming software is a monumental undertaking. As a result, Siri's developers—alongside dictation software company Nuance Communications—have programmed its voice recognition software to interpret commands and questions through a series of steps allowing people to interact with Siri in as human a way as possible."

Lagapa was a summer intern at Jameco Electronics. He is entering his sophomore year at UC Santa Cruz.

The Mercury Star is also a Wisdom Marking, which will be covered in the next chapter. Wisdom results only through *use* of this exceptional cleverness.

> STRENGTHS: My exceptional mental agility and ability to formulate quick conclusions make for a highly skilled strategist.
>
> PITFALL: Sneakiness, withholding information, cluelessness, vulnerability issues.
>
> MONEY MINDSET: I cleverly negotiate for top dollar for access to my gift of special ingenuity and highly complex code-cracking.
>
> BREAKTHROUGH QUESTIONS: In what settings does my quick wit increase my cash flow? How do I best apply my mental agility? *[Make note of this.]* Is my feedback loop open or closed most of the time? If open, who's in my think tank with me? If it's closed, who would make sense to have in my life as a sounding board?
>
> AFFIRMATION: "Wonder is the beginning of wisdom." —Socrates

Wisdom Markings

Employ These and Watch your Wealth Grow

> *"Bad weather always looks worse*
> *through a window"*
> —*Anonymous*

WISDOM COMES FROM discernment, insights, knowledge and *use* of logic. The key is to *use*, apply and employ knowledge for some designated outcome. Wisdom Markings are identified in the Wisdom Markings hand map (Figure 71) and described in the following section. Some Gift Markings and Head Lines (highlighted in bold), discussed in the previous chapters, are also Wisdom Markings. Be sure to take note in your journal or ear-mark pages with markings you see in your hands so you can complete the My Money Map Exercise at the end of the chapter.

For some people, using their wisdom can require taking great risk. Let's find out the specific risk required and the potential reluctance to take that gamble.

Ring of Solomon—The Detective

When you discover one or more arcs on the Mount of Jupiter (Figure 72), you'll find someone who has an unerring ability to understand human character. It's as if the owner has x-ray vision, able to see through the façade, through the bullshit. The more rings, the stronger the ability and most likely a theme in one's life.

According to Lifehack's "10 Proven Ways to Judge a Person's Character," the secret to evaluating personality is to reserve judgment and take your time. Observe others in certain situations; look at how they

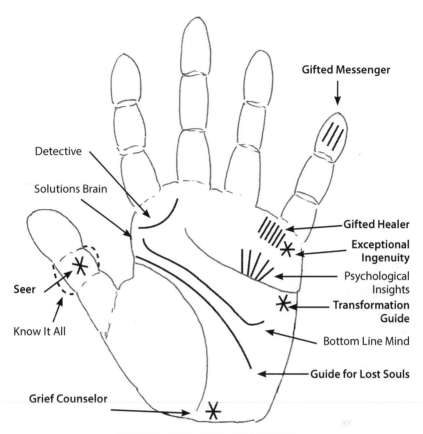

FIGURE 71: WISDOM MARKINGS.
GIFT MARKINGS THAT ARE ALSO WISDOM
MARKINGS ARE SHOWN IN BOLD.

react. Listen to them talking, joking, laughing, explaining, complaining, blaming, praising, ranting and preaching. Only then will you be able to judge their character. To the Detective, this all comes quite naturally, without lengthy assessment.

The wisdom comes forth as knowledge and insightful information are used to provide counsel. However, illuminating the truth can be viewed as judgmental, attacking or too revealing by the receiver and thus be rejected. With skill, the Detective, (a.k.a the B.S. Detector) will corral someone to see the truth, for their own good and/or the good of the people around. For example, the counselor tactfully tells the bulimic that she is avoiding and rejecting all feelings through her

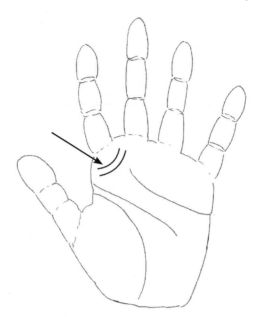

FIGURE 72: THE DETECTIVE

eating disorder, encouraging her to make improvement by learning to feel all of her feelings.

Solomon was the biblical king most famous for his wisdom. Perhaps the best-known story of his wisdom is the Judgment of Solomon: two women each lay claim to being the mother of the same child. Solomon easily resolved the dispute by commanding the child to be cut in half and shared between the two. One woman promptly renounced her claim, proving that she would rather give the child up than see it killed. Solomon declared the woman who showed compassion to be the true mother, entitled to the whole child. 1 Kings 3:16–28

While I didn't see her hands, Pamela Meyer who spoke on Ted Talk "How to Spot a Liar" and wrote *Liespotting: Proven Techniques to Detect Deception*, may have this glyph in one or both of her hands. Four to six lines or arcs on this mount would point to a private detective, police investigator, interrogator in the CIA or liespotting consulting for retail businesses. Another example of deception-detecting is Patrick Jane, lead character in the TV series *The Mentalist*. Jane uses his highly developed observation skills, previously employed to "read" people's minds as a psychic, to solve crimes as a consultant for the California Bureau of Investigation.

On the positive side, the Ring of Solomon belongs to someone who is motivated for the good of all concerned and has a high spiritual IQ. They love to learn, tell the truth and communicate with authority, harnessing the archetypal Jupiter energies. The downside possibility is reluctance to divulge their vision and understanding, perhaps for fear of being scorned.

The owner of the Ring of Solomon is good at perceiving. They see through the superficial to impart wisdom.

Potential positions include detective, investigator, teacher, social worker, parole officer, marketing specialists, human resource consultant, corporate trainer, novelist, sitcom script writer.

> STRENGTH: Unerring ability to understand human character—bringing forth insight into the nature of people.
>
> PITFALL: Powerless to disclose observations.
>
> MONEY MINDSET: Prosperity surrounds me as I take effective action based on my infinite wisdom.
>
> BREAKTHROUGH QUESTIONS: What comments have people made regarding my understanding of human character? Where and in what position would my natural insightful awareness be more revered and rewarded?
>
> AFFIRMATION: "The question isn't who is going to let me; it's who is going to stop me." —Ayn Rand

Know It All

The middle section of the thumb is read to pronounce one's ability and style for perceiving and discerning. You'll read more details about the thumbs in a later chapter. Because the Know It All is a Wisdom Marking, it's included here.

Take your time to look closely at the thumb of someone who has a lot to say and is well versed in a variety of topics. If the middle section is plump, full and even wide (Figure 73), you've found someone who is built with extra examination and discrimination faculties. They research a wide range of topics with encyclopedic aptitudes.

The traditional definition for the Know It All is that they behave as if they know everything. The owner of this feature isn't necessarily arrogant about their gift; it's more of a matter of fact.

I have a friend who is a walking wealth of wisdom. There hasn't been a topic brought up in our social circle that she doesn't know something about. Before I noticed her Know It All overly large middle thumb zone, I was a bit put off because any time I or someone in the group would speak on a topic, she would chime in and elegantly take

FIGURE 73: KNOW-IT-ALL

over the conversation on the topic, mostly correcting misinformation. She's nothing short of an expert on countless topics. As soon as I noticed this distinctive feature in her hand, I immediately interrupted her and exclaimed, "You're a know it all!" A grin was instantly painted on her face and with a sparkle in her eye, she said, "I know!" "And if Sarah would have listened to me about how to effectively tame the feral cat, the cat wouldn't have run off!" Since verifying this quality in her hand and witnessing her joy of being acknowledged, I gladly listen to what she has to say, especially when it comes to learning about something I want to know.

The challenge for the Know It All is to find the right listening audience who will appreciate their gift of vision, perception and discernment. If their exceptional advice falls on deaf ears, and they keep quiet as a result, their inner critic will take over and drive them crazy with the incessant fault-finding.

Potential positions include producer, director, professor, retirement/estate planner, fact-checker, attorney, Siri (voice recognition on smart phones).

STRENGTH: Through due diligence I am an excellent critic.

PITFALL: Keeping quiet, self-criticism.

MONEY MINDSET: I stretch into sharing my extraordinary understanding with the right forum and am generously compensated.

BREAKTHROUGH QUESTIONS: What people or groups would most appreciate my encyclopedic abilities? How might refraining from being a constant Know It All serve others in my life?

AFFIRMATION: "I would rather die of passion than of boredom." —Vincent van Gogh

Psychological Insights

When short vertical lines fan up off the Heart Line toward the pinkie and ring fingers, you'll find someone with unique and profound psychological insights.

The owner of this marking is a natural counselor able to understand human dilemmas and help people move through confusing and

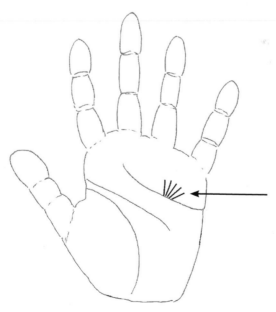

FIGURE 74: PSYCHOLOGICAL INSIGHTS

difficult times. He or she has just the right thing to say at precisely the right time. Listening, understanding and compassion are inherent skills.

While this marking would be helpful in any position, below are examples where psychological insights would be relied upon heavily.

Potential positions include social worker, school psychologist, intuitive, wellness practitioner, novelist, realtor.

STRENGTH: I humbly realize I am a master of insight, and I offer my services with delight.

PITFALL: Disregard of perceptiveness.

MONEY MINDSET: I gladly receive payment for my gift of insight, knowing the relief experienced through interaction with my abilities.

BREAKTHROUGH QUESTIONS: If I were to use my psychological insights mastery in a larger capacity, what would that look like? How could I double my income in the next year using my psychological insights?

AFFIRMATION: "I live in the now and am wide awake to my opportunities." —Florence Scovel Shinn

My Money Map Exercise

If you have three or more Gift and Wisdom Markings in your hands, locate the ones that are most eye-catching—the ones you have no doubt recognizing. They are calling out be used. Using the words in this book, describe the strengths and pitfalls linked to these markings. Also note the associated Money Mindsets. (See the example on page 60.)

The Gift and Wisdom Markings I See in My Hands

Right Hand

PAGE: _____ MARKING: _____

STRENGTH: _____

_____

PITFALL: _____

_____

MONEY MINDSET: _____

_____

_____

Left Hand

PAGE: _____ MARKING: _____

STRENGTH: _____

_____

PITFALL: _____

_____

MONEY MINDSET: _____

_____

_____

Note the markings you see in both hands on the blank
hand maps at the back of this book, pages 212–213.

The Thumb

Your Engine for Success

> *"The most dangerous risk of all: The risk of spending your life not doing what you want on the bet you can buy yourself the freedom to do it later."*
> —Alan Watts

WHEN CONSIDERING OUR money habits and goals we must consider the entire condition of our thumb. This single digit is instrumental for getting results by contemplating dreams, discernment skills, self-discipline and applying one's will. Vernon Mahabal, author of *The Secret Code on Your Palm*, says, "Our palm and fingers contain our talents and abilities. Our thumb is like the engine or power station that can make those talents come to life."

Following are thumb factors to consider when analyzing your hands.

- Size, length, back view
- Sections
- The angle of opposition
- The set of the thumb
- Flexibility
- Curvature
- Tips
- Glyphs

Imagine for a moment not having your thumbs. What could you get done without your thumbs? Because we have thumbs, we are able to rearrange living room furniture, grocery stores shelves, road systems and jungles. Thumbs belong to people of all ages, so we see infants grab bottles, teens grip steering wheels, adults building homes and business people constructing shopping malls and warehouses. All ages imagine a dream, discern and reach results in very different ways.

Thumb Variables

How you shape, control and govern your world can be interpreted by the characteristics of your thumbs. Your ability to get things done can be analyzed by many variables in your thumbs. For example, big thumbs equate to big doings and small thumbs are happy doing less. No thumb is better than another. The power lies in understanding strengths for success and potential challenges to address and improve.

Key words for the thumb: Results, outcomes, determination, will-power, vitality, doing, accomplishment, assertiveness, persistence and manifestation.

The following thumb variables will tell you a great deal about your capability to use the qualities inscribed in other areas of your hands. For example, recall Figure 11, Super Responsible (long, straight Fate Line climbing up to the base of the middle finger), when I mentioned a large and low-set thumb will maximize how one is driven and com-mitted with stellar results. Conversely, a small thumb, held tightly to the hand will minimize the extent of the A+ qualities.

At the end of this chapter, you'll be guided to identify various at-tributes you see in your thumbs based on what you learn here, and complete the My Money Map Exercise. Plan to blend the qualities of your thumbs with other patterns you have identified in your hands to maximize your strengths and mend your weaknesses. Let's make your talents come to life!

Size of Thumb

To evaluate the size and length of the thumb, cover the thumb and visualize the type of thumb that would look appropriate on the hand. Uncover the thumb, then assess how suitable the thumb is for the hand it's plugged into. Ideally, a large hand has a correspondingly large sized thumb, not a small thumb.

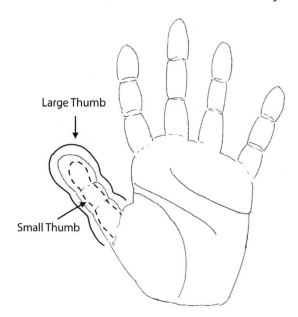

Large Thumb

Small Thumb

FIGURE 75: LARGE AND SMALL THUMBS

A large thumb relative to the hand belongs to someone capable of big results. They are outgoing, assertive and determined. Large thumbs indicate force of character. A thumb that is too big belongs to someone who is pompous, domineering, gruff, overbearing and bigoted, like the character Archie Bunker on "All in the Family" or chief enforcer Darth Vader in *Star Wars*.

A small thumb in relation to the hand belongs to someone who is easygoing, quiet, passive, reserved, shy, perhaps timid and challenged to complete things. People with small thumbs have less force for doing. Small-thumbed individuals are ruled by sympathy. They prefer to follow instead of lead.

A thumb that is too small, like that of a chimpanzee, could find day-to-day life overwhelming. The owner feels best with less responsibility. Effects of people and circumstances weigh heavily on them.

A long thumb (Figure 76), again relative to the size of the hand and fingers, takes time to deliberate carefully. A short thumb (dotted line) indicates someone who acts quickly.

The length of the Head Line should also be considered with the length of the thumb. A long thumb with a long Head Line will spend even more time deliberating and synthesizing information. A short

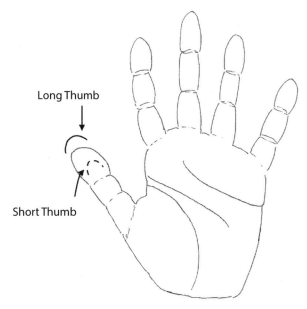

FIGURE 76: LONG AND SHORT THUMBS

thumb with a short Head Line will both think and act quickly. Keep in mind, a hand with a short thumb could also have a long Head Line. This combination will balance more time spent thinking before taking the quick action.

Summary of Size and Length: Size shows the available energy for doing and manifesting in the world. Large thumbs are built to do more. They try to shape events and do well having big jobs. Smaller thumbs won't do well with large loads placed on them. Long thumbs like to spend time deliberating, while short thumbs act quickly.

Back View of Thumb

When observing the thumb from the back, looking directly at the nail side, look for the following:

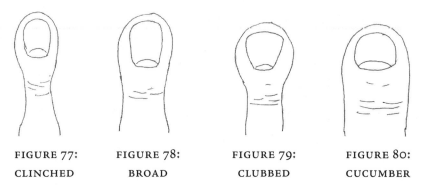

FIGURE 77:   FIGURE 78:   FIGURE 79:   FIGURE 80:
CLINCHED   BROAD   CLUBBED   CUCUMBER

Cinched: A cinched thumb, as if enfolded by a corset, belongs to someone who is tactful. They know what to say, when and how to say it.

Broad: When the thumb looks healthy and is broader than the cinched thumb, the owner rises over obstacles. The determination is strong and backed by physical strength.

Clubbed: Old palmistry books designate a thick and rounded or broad and thick thumb tip with a short nail as the "murderer's thumb." The owner will display varying degrees of stubbornness and potentially a violent temper, depending on the other qualities of the hand it's plugged into. The rest of the hand must be assessed to determine how explosive the owner will be. Smooth skin texture, pink colored skin and a full Mount of Venus (ball of the thumb) will soften the "beastly impulse." Course skin texture, hard hands, red skin, a stiff inflexible thumb will exaggerate potential violent tendencies. I've met two individuals with clubbed thumbs and neither was violent, as far as I know. Both are in marriages lasting over forty years, which would seem to suggest ability to get along—and not murder.

Cucumber: A thumb devoid of any symmetry looks like a cucumber. The owner is heavy in his or her action, potentially even uses brute force in life and brute passion in love. The owner can be seen as blunt, tactless and unreasoning. They know it all and tell others what to do.

Back View Summary: the range of behavior moves from tactful (cinched) to tactless (cucumber).

Sections of the Thumb

The thumb, as well as the fingers, is broken into three worlds: abstract and conceptual (upper), practical and mental (middle) and instinctual and sensory (lower). William Benham, author of *The Laws of Scientific Hand Reading* said, "These three worlds of the thumb embody three qualities supremely important to the success of any human being, and they may justly be classed among the greatest moving forces in the entire category of human levers. Without them no amount of brilliance or talent, no amount of scholarly attainment, will enable a subject to achieve great success."

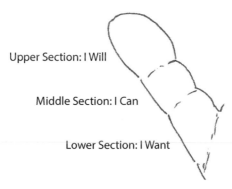

Upper Section: I Will

Middle Section: I Can

Lower Section: I Want

FIGURE 81: SECTIONS OF THE THUMB

Upper Section: The upper section of the thumb is called the zone of "I will." The will gives us the drive to act. If the upper section, looking from the palm side, is longest relative to the other sections of the thumb, the owner gets results through personal willpower. If it's overly large the owner appears willful, dominated by ego. The upper section of the thumb corresponds to the crown chakra, where we connect with heavenly wisdom. Remembering to align with higher wisdom can increase success.

Horizontal lines through the tip of the thumb indicate worry and fret. Worry and looking for things that can go wrong will undoubtedly interrupt the flow of financial freedom. If fret lines appear on the upper section of your thumb, find ways to relax and trust in the process of life. What you focus on grows.

Middle Section: The middle section of the thumb is related to discernment, reason, evaluation, judgment and planning. The mind checks through sifting and rationalizing information. This section of the thumb is associated with "I can." When the middle section of the thumb is longer than either the top or bottom section, the person makes a good planner and they like to make their intelligence known. Their willpower is guided by a reasoning brain. This portion of the thumb correlates to the third-eye chakra, where we have the power to "see" from a more accurate perspective.

Ability to make choices with clarity comes easily when the middle section is longest, unless horizontal lines cross this zone of discernment. These lines act like log jams and impede the flow of decision-making. Money making strategies must include expert counsel from trusted advisors when multiple lines lie across this segment of the thumb. I also advise clients with this configuration to double-check their bookkeeper's work. Unsurprisingly, I've heard stories about funds being misappropriated by family members and financial advisors who were improperly evaluated—or not at all. Trust but verify.

Lower Section: The lowest section of the thumb closest to the ball, where the thumb is attached to the hand, exemplifies results through feeling, imagination, vision, instincts, self-expression and speaking up. This section of the thumb is associated with "I want." If the lowest section of the thumb is longest the owner will be keen on creating visions based on their imagination and desires. This part of the thumb is related to the throat chakra, and when longest, implies the person would readily speak up about what they dream about and want.

When this section is shortest, I ask my client, "What's your wildest dream?" My job as the financial freedom hand reader is to encourage revealing the dream, not keeping it a secret.

Summary of Sections: Another way to consider the zones of the thumb is that each section correlates to ready (bottom), aim (middle) and fire (upper). The bottom says, "I dream of taking a vacation to the beach" (concentration, desires, expression through voice). The middle says, "I'll look at the calendar, check the bank account, then decide" (brings intelligence to the dream). The upper says, "Let's go!" (wills the action). Look for the longest section of your thumb to determine

your strengths and the shortest section for your weakness. For example, if you have a short middle section you may not take much time
to "aim" before you "fire." Therefore, you'll get better outcomes when
you spend extra time aiming (discerning and planning) before firing
(taking action).

While it's rare, a thumb can have only two sections. This indicates
a person having a voice and wanting it to be heard! Blurting out information is not uncommon. One person with two sections on her thumb
told me, "I'm not a blurter, I'm a belter on stage—as a jazz singer."

Angle of Opposition

The splay of the thumb away from the hand (Figure 82) indicates the
sphere of influence the owner feels most comfortable inhabiting. To see
the natural angle of the thumb, shake your hands and hold them in the
air facing you, or place them palm side down on a flat surface. Notice
the position of the thumb in relation to the hand. The splay displays
different styles of self-reliance, confidence and productiveness.

Next, you'll learn about tight, medium and wide angles of opposition.

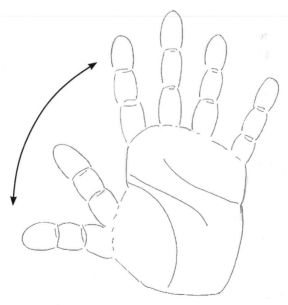

FIGURE 82: THUMB ANGLES OF OPPOSITION

Tight Angle of Opposition: When the thumb is naturally held tight-ly into the hand, close to the index finger, the owner is comfortable with less to do, they keep to themselves, are private and feel discomfort around other people. The owner of a thumb held tight to the hand will tend to keep people at arm's length. They complete tasks best when left alone, but actually don't want much responsibility at all.

If your thumb is found most often nestled up to your hand, you withdraw easily, can feel depressive, insecure and helpless. Perhaps you're consciously giving space for deep introspection or recovering from abuse. Your money success story will improve with an increased dose of confidence and willingness to be seen more often than you feel comfortable with. Another approach is to perform in a role behind the scenes, requiring minimal interaction with groups of co-workers. You'll also want a solid strategy to handle one problem at a time.

Someone in a coma will most likely have a thumb tucked into the palm of the hand. This indicates a person who is completely withdrawn from the outer world.

Medium Angle of Opposition: When the thumb is held away from the hand at about 45° to 70°, you'll find someone with lots of initiative who can be self-employed or employed by others. They operate with sense of ease and balance. They enjoy being with others but will not like being controlled by others. The owner responds in responsible and sensible ways working individually or with groups.

Wide Angle of Opposition: When the thumb is held at a 90° angle of opposition away from the hand, we find a high achiever. The cap-tain, general and CEO most likely have thumbs held away from the hands. This person is comfortable and confident with large territories to manage and influence. Like Oprah Winfrey, they are a shaper of the environment they are in. This owner is confident and self-reliant. Operating an international business where the world is their territo-ry to embrace would be something quite comfortable for this person. Without a large region to manage they get bored or antsy. Without a proper outlet for their incredible initiative they'll feel internally inept.

Angle of Opposition Summary: The angle of opposition is the phrase used to describe how the thumb is naturally placed next to or away from the hand. This distance between the thumb and the hand shows the size of territory the owner would like to govern, to embrace, to hold, control and influence. The angle, or splay, shows different styles of self-sufficiency and industriousness. The angle can change depending on the environment the person is in. For example, a trainer of airplane mechanics will display a wide angle when he or she is in the front of the classroom lecturing. When the trainer must sit in an audience the angle may become tight.

Thumb Set

The set of the thumb is identified by the location where the thumb inserts into the palm. The set of the thumb shows the innate capacity to get things done. Thumb sets are identified as very high, high, medium and low set.

FIGURE 83: THUMB SETS

Very High Set: When the insertion (bone structure) of the thumb is very high up on the palm, close to the base of the index finger, the thumb cannot oppose the digits. More effort is required to get results. Getting many things done is difficult. The monkey's paw is the closest to that of the human thumb. Monkeys' thumbs are set high on the side of the paw and don't have the ability to oppose the other digits, and therefore primarily peel bananas and don't have what's required to rearrange the jungle.

High Set: A high-set thumb typically belongs to someone who has minimal ability to adapt to circumstances. The owner does well at sorting mail and other simple tasks. They must work harder to get results. The destiny of a high set thumb can be to start a business. If this is the case, then the founder must work extra hours above and beyond what a medium or low-set thumb would do to get the company up and running. The good news is, hard work pays off. The bad news is, frustration reduces self-worth.

Medium Set: When the thumb is plugged into the palm about midway between the wrist and the start of the Head Line, the owner will have average capability to accomplish. He or she is balanced in his or her undertakings and is properly cautious in his or her endeavors.

Low Set: When the insertion point of the thumb is low on the palm, near the bottom of the hand, nearly parallel with the wrist, we'll find somebody who has a great ability for results. This thumb points away from the hand and creates a wide opening from the index finger. They are confident and it's easy for them to get things done. This is a do-it-yourself person who will do best with troops and minions to help them follow through for bigger results. At their best, success comes through leaving details to skilled staff. The bad news possibility is not deciding which direction to take, and squandering their riches. Children with low-set thumbs are selling lemonade in front of the house as little kid entrepreneurs by the time they are five years old.

Thumb Set Summary: The high-, medium- or low-set thumb reveals the natural ability to get things done. Thumbs set higher on the hand typically work harder for results than thumbs set lower on the hand.

Flexibility

Flexibility of the thumb shows how the owner will be influenced by the world. To measure the flexibility, from the tip of the thumb, gently push it away from the hand. In general, a flexible thumb belongs to somebody who is able to bend and move when they are tried by the influences of the world. They are adaptable, generous and emotional. If it's too flexible, the owner gets easily side-tracked, is challenged to follow through, can be extravagant and a bit of a spendthrift. To the contrary, a stiff thumb, minimal give when tested, indicates someone who is rigid and firm, not so flexible in action. They stick to the plan, are practical and have common sense. When it's unbendable the owner is stubborn and despises change. He or she can be stingy, cautious and reserved, with overwhelming requirements for self-control. The unbendable thumb belongs to someone who only trusts themselves.

Flexible thumbs are like willow trees that easily bend with the wind. People with bendable thumbs are adaptable. Stiff thumbs are like oak trees with deep roots, less affected by the wind. People with rigid thumbs are less flexible.

Thumb Curvature

When the thumb is sitting naturally, at rest, see if it's straight or curved. You don't need to push on the thumb to determine the curvature. The straight thumb belongs to somebody who is ruled by reason. It matters how he or she thinks. Logic outweighs emotion when it comes to goals. Conversely, a curved thumb is ruled by emotions. It matters how he or she feels, and action is symbiotic with changing emotions.

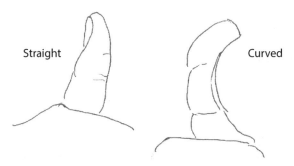

Straight   Curved

FIGURE 84: THUMB CURVATURE

Thumb Tip Types

The thumb tip type shows preference and approach in using the energy of the thumb. Look at the face of your thumb and notice how the tip is shaped. Most tips are round.

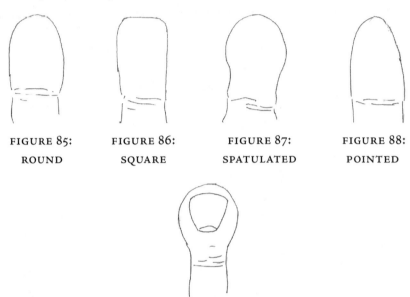

| FIGURE 85: | FIGURE 86: | FIGURE 87: | FIGURE 88: |
| ROUND | SQUARE | SPATULATED | POINTED |

FIGURE 79: CLUBBED TIP

Round tips, also called conic, show an individual who generally desires harmony and wants to get along with others. Achievements will generally be hampered in environments involving conflict and opposition.

Flat and square tips require practicality, precision and reason in getting results. Wishy-washy or highly imaginative environments will aggravate people with flat thumb tips.

Spatulated tips accomplish best through originality, variety and individuality. Results will not come through conformity.

Pointed tips are drawn to using imagination. This can contradict the determination of the thumb and make it more difficult to get desired outcomes. The owner will do best in a job where their dreams run free with minimal requirements for completion.

Clubbed tips (like a ping pong paddle) belong to people who can be explosive because the fullness of the upper section of "will" gets clogged. When the energy clogs it can blow unexpectedly. When the tip is wide and bulbous and the nail is short, the owner will be more successful as they develop the skill of learning to count to ten before reacting.

Glyphs on the Thumb

While it is uncommon to have a star on any section of the thumb, go ahead and check. If you have this special imprint on any of the three sections on the thumb, it's important to know and employ the meaning so that you can boost your revenue-generating opportunities.

Star of Intention

The Star of Intention is a six-pointed asterisk located on the inside, lower area of the upper section of the thumb. This is the zone of "will."

This glyph belongs to a human dynamo who can manifest results very quickly through setting intentions, provided they believe in themselves. The owner is capable of manifesting just about anything he or she desires. Vision board contents immediately come to life as the

FIGURE 89: STAR OF INTENTION

pictures are pieced together on the canvas, or simply in their mind's eye. The owner constantly manifests their thoughts, positive or negative, because either way they will come to fruition.

STRENGTH: As a real go-getter, my visions (with or without a vision board) are realized immediately.

PITFALL: Missing the point of power, bullheaded.

MONEY MINDSET: I intend. It happens. Bam!

BREAKTHROUGH QUESTIONS: What's on my recent list of accomplishments? Which outcomes have been most significant? Do I believe in myself and my abilities for big accomplishments? If not, what specific thoughts will I transform? On a scale from 0–5 (5 being most) how clear am I about my money goals?

AFFIRMATION: "It's not about what it is. It's about what it can become." —Dr. Seuss

Seer Star

The Seer Star is a six-pointed asterisk in the inside middle section of the thumb. This zone is associated with logic.

This tiny pattern belongs to someone who has exceptional perception, insight and discernment skills. He or she can see into reality using their third eye, also called the spiritual eye. Success comes as the individual allows what she "sees" to be used in her work or business. When the eye is blocked, meaning the gift isn't being engaged, the owner will feel unfulfilled. Read more about the Seer Star in the section on Gift Markings (page 133).

FIGURE 63: SEER STAR

Singer Star

The Singer Star is a six-pointed asterisk in the inside bottom section of the thumb.

This person would do well generating revenue using their voice. The owner has some sort of special communications to do. Examples include radio, voiceover, audio book reading or singing to an audience. If you have a six-pointed asterisk in this section of the thumb and money issues are dominating your consciousness, here's the way out: use your talent for creative self-expression through your voice.

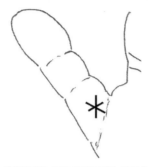

FIGURE 90: SINGER STAR

STRENGTH: My voice is attractive, and my message matters.

PITFALL: Blocked dreams, suppression of speech.

MONEY MINDSET: Currency floods to me as my voice carries through the airwaves.

BREAKTHROUGH QUESTIONS: My wildest dream is....

_____

_____

Do I acknowledge compliments about my voice? Where is my favorite place to sing? Where does my voice want to be revealed?

AFFIRMATION: "The only thing better than singing is more singing." —Ella Fitzgerald

My Money Map Exercise

Use the following checklist to highlight elements you see in your right thumb based on what you read. We use both thumbs in business, but the right hand is typically the hand to read for results out in the world. However, examine both right and left thumbs for stars. While reading thumbs is very new for you, do your best to select and circle (below) the traits you see. If you can't decide, simply move to the next characteristic on the list.

For the features you do see, circle the associated description, and list one or two key words, either strengths or weaknesses. Let's optimize your strategy for financial freedom.

CHARACTERISTIC   DESCRIPTION   KEY WORDS

SIZE: Big | Medium | Small _____

LENGTH: Long | Average | Short _____

LONG SECTION: Upper | Middle | Bottom _____

SHORT SECTION: Upper | Middle | Bottom _____

SET: High | Medium | Low _____

FLEXIBILITY: Very Flexible | Flexible | Stiff _____

CURVATURE: Curved | Straight _____

TIP TYPE: Round | Square | Spatulate | Pointed _____

GLYPH/STAR: Intention (will) | Seer (discernment) |
                 Singer (voice) _____

Note the markings you see in both hands
on the blank hand maps at the back of this book, pages 212–213.

Hand Shape Basics

Your Archetypal Approach to the World

"Rich people see every dollar as a 'seed' that can be planted to earn a hundred more dollars, which can then be replanted to earn a thousand more dollars."

—*T. Harv Eker*

BY NOW YOU are catching on to the fact that no one in the world has hands just like yours. You're seeing the various aspects of the hands and understanding the fundamental components that make up the money map etched into your hands. Now you're ready to look at the basic shape and other characteristics of your hands that reveal your persona and style of behavior. Personality and character are naturally exposed through patterns of action and preferences in relating to the world. Recognizing the meaning of your hand shape can illuminate and help you understand your personality traits and aid you in claiming positive aspects of yourself and making personal improvements. If financial gain is your aim, your hand shape types must be employed in accordance to how they're built—Earth (productive,) Air (logical), Water (sensitive), Fire (magnetic).

One's personality presents distinct archetypal patterns around money, family, goals, life, death and more. Archetypes reflect recurring styles of thought and behavior. Think of a gambler, hero, jester, humanitarian or outlaw; each displays attributes consistent with particular beliefs and interior narratives. These narratives create filters and operate unconsciously—all the time. Archetypal filters are like lenses we see through when making decisions. Therefore, the more we become aware of these patterns, the more we can change our unconscious behaviors and make powerful choices for creating and keeping more money. You'll also learn what and how you prefer to give, be it money, time, conversation, care, ideas, things etc.

Think of each element (earth, air, water and fire) as an archetype. More complex archetypes can be recognized in the hands, but they're beyond the scope of this book. For now, we'll keep it simple and look at each elemental archetype to understand exactly why they operate the way they do.

Your two hands might be shaped similarly, or you might have one shape on one hand and another shape on the other hand. Hands rarely contain only one element. Usually they have several, and sometimes all the elements. The shape of your right hand indicates your approach to the outer world; the shape of your left hand reveals your behavior at home or in private.

You will recognize the hand shape types more quickly with practice. Be patient with yourself. Let your eye look for the various aspects that correspond to the basic hand shape types.

Steps for Reading Hand Shape

Step 1: Shape. Determine whether the palm is square or broad (Earth), long and rectangular like a shoebox (Air), long and narrow (Water), or rounded, pear-shaped or irregular (Fire).

Step 2: Fingers. Relative to the length of the palm, notice whether the fingers are short and thick (Earth), long and straight (Air), long and thin like seaweed (Water), or longer than Earth but not as long as Air (Fire).

Step 3: Lines. See whether the line formations are few and deeply chiseled (Earth), many and thin (Air), many and baby fine (Water), or many and sharp (Fire).

Step 4: Skin. Check to see whether the skin is coarse with thick corrugations (Earth), smooth (Air), baby smooth (Water), or dry as though it needs lotion (Fire).

You may have noticed that steps 3 and 4 don't relate to the shape of the hand. When analyzing the hands to determine their elemental profiles and the associated personae, we also consider the lines on the palm and characteristics of the skin.

ELEMENT	SHAPE	FINGERS	LINES	SKIN
Earth	Square, broad	Short, thick	Chiseled, few	Coarse
Air	Long, shoebox	Long, straight	Thin, many	Smooth
Water	Narrow, long	Long, thin, seaweed	Tiny, fine, many	Fine, smooth
Fire	Irregular, rounded	Longer than Earth, straight	Sharp, crackling	Dry

The Primary Hand Shapes

Earth—Productive

The Earth hand has a square or broad palm. The fingers are shorter than the palm. The Earth hand has the shortest finger length of the four hand types. This hand is heavy, solid, coarse, and typically marked with very few lines. The few lines include deeply chiseled Heart, Life and Head Lines and are clear to see. Sometimes you'll also see a Fate Line running vertically up the center of the hand. The skin ridges are well defined, and the thumb is usually stiff. Both men and woman can own this hand type.

Think about the earth. Consider the ground that you stand on. The earth is solid, dependable, and reliable. Jump up and you'll surely land back on the ground. The earth supports us with food and shelter. It appears motionless on the surface, but underneath its thin crust the earth is alive, with great potential for eruption. Colossal pressures keep the plates of the earth in place, but on occasion they move with tremendous fury. Beneath its surface is fertilizer for life. Because of what the earth provides, it is considered productive and protective.

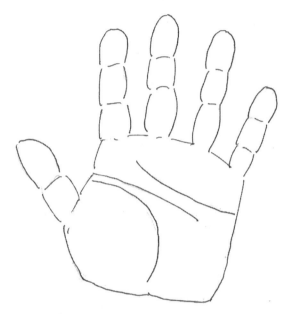

FIGURE 91: EARTH HAND SHAPE—PRODUCTIVE

You'll find people with Earth hands building things, holding tools, doing carpentry, crafting, and possibly massaging necks and shoulders. Owners of square hands like to get dirty and love to do labor such as farming, sculpting, and solving problems with hard work and exertion. They have a love of the outdoors.

If the physical landscape of your hands is square with short fingers and few deeply carved lines, you may feel as though you carry the weight of the world on your shoulders. You can easily dismiss someone who doesn't demonstrate what you consider the "right" degree of loyalty. You have a few high-quality friendships which have taken years to develop. Your thinking is practical, and expressing feelings is uncomfortable (and perhaps unnecessary). You keep things simple, are slow to change, and think in black and white and absolutes. You take pleasure in tactile contact with things like tools, products, animals and soil.

If you work with an Earth-handed person, you'll be wise to recognize and support his or her values of privacy, honor, loyalty, security, and hard work. You might hear him or her say, "My word is
my bond." Give this person space to work on projects, and allow him
or her time to tinker. Your Earth friend despises the fact that when
products such as dishwashers break, consumers rush out and buy new
ones instead of fixing the old ones. If you break through the Earth
surface with disregard for the Earth-handed person's values of conservation, practicalities and loyalty, you may see destructive energies
erupt.

Potential positions include laborer, logger, farmer, construction
worker, mason, massage therapist, mail carrier, caregiver.

> STRENGTH: I am rooted in consistency, integrity, tradi-
> tion and simplicity.
>
> PITFALL: Complete emotional detachment, inflexibility.
>
> MONEY MINDSET: I am paid handsomely for my strong
> sense of loyalty, protective instincts, commonsense
> nature, and the strength of my hands.
>
> BREAKTHROUGH QUESTIONS: How is the world I carry
> on my shoulders benefiting my bank account? How is
> my pragmatic approach helping and hindering my rela-
> tionships at home and in business?
>
> AFFIRMATION: "The four winds of success now blow my
> way. From North, South, East and West comes my end-
> less good." —Florence Scovel Shinn

Air—Logical

The Air hand has a rectangular palm with straight fingers that are
longer than the Earth and Fire fingers. Look for a shoebox shape of
the hand and fingers. The skin is smoother than that of Earth and Fire
hands. There are usually many lines in the Air palm, but they are thin-
ner than the crackling lines of the Fire palm and not as deep.

Think of the air that flows, swirls, twirls, and spins around us every
day. Air is essential for carrying information from point A to point B.

The sounds of the voices of two people move on invisible airwaves. Things, ideas, sounds, scents and people connect in and through air. In short, air enables highly complex forms of communication such as speech, and even dog whistles undetectable to the human ear. High in

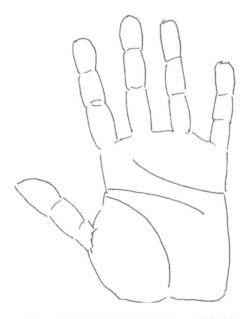

FIGURE 92: AIR HAND SHAPE—LOGICAL

the sky, invisible to the eye, air can also turn into wind, cutting into the path of airplanes in route to their destinations.

You'll most likely find people with Air hands engaged in cerebral activity. They streamline information. Politics, debates, theorizing, educating, writing, reporting, unraveling mental knots, and mediating relations between people are activities they may enjoy. Ideal work must include something to analyze, understand and communicate.

If you have an Air hand, you have a gift for observation and an eye for detail. You are keenly aware of words, sounds, body language, and subtle communication. You enjoy complex forms of communication and are quick-witted. Thinking, translating and transmitting messages are right up your alley. As long as you cultivate an appropriate level of sensitivity, you can be an excellent mediator. When others don't appear to understand the workings of your mind, you can be quickly irritated, responding with judgment, closed-mindedness, aloofness or drama.

If you work with an Air-handed person, you'll be wise to keep an open mind, take part in debate, and not take the Air hand's occasional sarcasm personally. Realize he or she is curious and motivated by information.

Potential positions include debater, politician, principal, teacher, researcher, journalist, orator, writer, analyst, investigator.

> STRENGTH: I have an agile mind with the ability to examine, see and comprehend from different perspectives.

> PITFALL: Sarcasm, fault-finding, overly critical of self and others.

> MONEY MINDSET: My active mind, clarity in thought, and intellect are highly valued and given due compensation.

> BREAKTHROUGH QUESTIONS: How does seeking to understand before being understood best serve me and others? What revelatory idea could increase my revenue of riches?

> AFFIRMATION: "I give thanks for my whirlwind success." —Florence Scovel Shinn

Water—Sensitive

The Water hand has a long and narrow palm, with long, thin, wavy fingers that resemble seaweed. The skin is silky smooth, with many fine lines in the palm. The Water hand is often soft and flexible. The Head Line frequently curves downward toward the lower area of the palm.

Water is fluid and calm when contained. It takes the shape of its container. At the same time, water seeks to escape through evaporation, and after rising it falls back to the surface as dew or rain. Water can be deceptive with its calm surface, as strong currents and deep turbulence may swirl below. The sea is often unpredictable, and it is capable of unleashing destructive forces.

Water droplets come together to form bonds. A pool of water reflects its surroundings like a mirror. The famous martial artist Bruce Lee was often quoted as saying, "Be like the water." He taught his students to adapt and mold themselves to their opponents. When you find a Water hand, you'll see someone who can blend into her surroundings

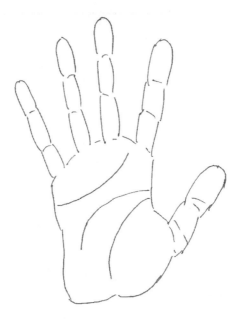

FIGURE 93: WATER HAND SHAPE—SENSITIVE

like a chameleon and conform to the needs of others. Maintaining calm seas is a primary objective of this fluid soul. You'll find Water types writing poetry, engaging in creative arts, ad-lib acting, mothering and keeping the home peaceful.

If the narrow, long and sensitive Water hand belongs to you, you are motivated by emotional connections, an exceptional listener, and can offer caring counsel. You'll want a job that's more than a paycheck. You quickly absorb and reflect stronger, more dominant personalities, as well as those that are irritable or moody. Because external feelings and moods often distract you, paying attention to everyday details such as balancing your checkbook may not be your strong suit. Without taking into account other variables in your hands, you'd do best to avoid work involving hitting sales targets, confrontation and hectic environments. You may find yourself worrying excessively that you said the "wrong" thing. You should carefully consider your boundaries, so that you don't devote yourself to filling up the many containers longing for your care. Allow yourself ample time to daydream. Follow your intuition.

If you work with someone with a Water hand with baby-fine skin, be sensitive to the emotions that stir him or her deeply. Because bonding is so important, disconnect gently. His or her mood changes according to the moods of people around him or her, so allow for his or her adaptable and changeable nature, which may vary according to all aspects of the environment, including people, places and things.

Potential positions include poet, musician, actor, psychic, photographer, therapist, ballet dancer, social worker, life coach, copywriter, graphic designer.

> STRENGTH: My empathetic, intuitive and nurturing nature makes me a natural diplomat.
>
> PITFALL: Emotional drama, boundary issues.
>
> MONEY MINDSET: I am appreciated and highly compensated for my eye for detail, compassion, care and sensitivity to the needs of others.
>
> BREAKTHROUGH QUESTION: How would saying "no" in any particular situation surge my financial flow? If I were to be in a healthy, cooperative and truly beneficial environment, where would that be? How can I bring more calm and joy to my current work environment?
>
> AFFIRMATION: "I see clearly and act quickly and my greatest expectations come to pass in a miraculous way." —Florence Scovel Shinn

Fire—Magnetic

The Fire hand has a rounded and longish palm, with many lines criss-crossing the palm. The shape of this hand may look irregular, like that of an apple or pear. It has shorter fingers relative to the length of the palm than the Air and Water shapes, but not as short as those of the square Earth hand. The skin may look and feel dry. Many deep, sharp, energetic lines cover the palm, as if slashed with Zorro's sword. These lines display the liveliness and passion of their owner.

Consider the qualities of fire. Flames are mesmerizing. Fire excites and delights our mind, body and soul. Fire gives and takes energy from its surroundings. People like to sit around a campfire to keep warm and have fun, but fire can be destructive when uncontrolled. Fire is active,

FIGURE 94: FIRE HAND SHAPE—MAGNETIC

spontaneous, untamed, attractive, and on display. Fire dies out when a lid or a wet blanket covers it.

The owner of a Fire hand likely acts on impulse and instinct. He or she may not look before leaping. One owner of a Fire hand told me, "I react, say things, and think later." The challenge of a Fire-handed person is to demonstrate exuberance in balance: neither too much nor too little, but "just right." Just right is measured by internal requirements, not by what is acceptable to the outside world.

You'll find Fire types in any field of action, expressing their creativity and often taking the lead. They are typically enthusiastic Jacks-of-all-trades, solving problems intuitively rather than intellectually.

If Zorro has made his marks on your hands, be a catalyst for change with the zest and zeal that come naturally to you. Give yourself permission to live with passion, allowing your flame to glow. You have places to be, people to see, and things to do. Slow down enough to finish projects, and finish one at a time. Details and practicalities are probably not your thing. While delegating may come easily to you, there are some things that need your personal attention.

If you work with a Fire type, don't restrict her passion by imposing routine or regularity. If she appears unreliable in her multiplicity, realize she is simply allowing her creativity to flow. She is motivated by impulse and variety. She won't like to conform to deadlines because deadlines restrict possibility. If you impose required expectations, you may soon witness a wildfire to contend with. Give her colorful flames space and time to blaze. Allow her to multitask. Her magnetism and enthusiasm thrive through many creative channels.

Potential positions include artist/creator, marketing consultant, comedian, camp director, Montessori teacher, party planner, clown, disk jockey, concierge, chef, sports coach, bartender, flight attendant, hair stylist.

> STRENGTH: I am extremely creative, can pour on the charisma, and my enthusiasm keeps the momentum going for the team and the boss.

> PITFALL: Task incompletion, excessive changeability.

> MONEY MINDSET: In the right setting, my spirited nature and a sense of joyful accomplishment are applauded with big bucks.

> BREAKTHROUGH QUESTIONS: What one unfinished project would increase my monetary reservoir the most after it's completed? Is my current employment, position or boss stifling my spark and thrashing my pizazz? If so, what can be done about it? In what revenue-generating arena is my creative flair most respected and rewarded?

> AFFIRMATION: "I am harmonious, poised and magnetic." —Florence Scovel Shinn

Blending Hand Shapes

Now that you have explored the four basic hand shapes, you must realize that many hands do not conform to one shape. In fact, most hands blend two hand shapes. You might see long straight fingers (Air) on a square palm (Earth), or an irregular palm (Fire) with short, thick fingers (Earth), and so on. Identify the two most prominent elements, and blend key points of both elements together. Note both the strengths and pitfalls of each element to better understand how a person with a blended hand shape can live with more balance.

Identifying the traits associated with your own hand shape will help you to better understand what motivates you to act and communicate as you do. If you ignore your elemental characteristics, you deny pieces of yourself, and life becomes difficult. As an example, if you have Air and Fire in your hands, you need to observe and communicate (Air) with energetic flair (Fire), like a powerful workshop leader. If you work in a setting that doesn't support your essential style of behavior, you end up feeling confused and empty. Knowing about and claiming your true traits and making your preferences known to yourself and others will make a great you even better, because you'll be living your truth in your natural element.

Take a moment now to identify the primary shapes of your hands. Notice which elements you see most prominently. It sometimes helps to determine which elements you see least, and arrive at what is most important by process of elimination.

My Money Map Exercise

Using the words in the book, describe some of the key shapes and traits, strengths and pitfalls of your hand shapes. (See the example on page 60.)

The Hand Shapes I See in My Hands

Right Hand

PAGE: _____ SHAPE & TRAITS: _____

STRENGTH: _____

_____

PITFALL: _____

_____

MONEY MINDSET: _____

_____

_____

Left Hand

PAGE: _____ SHAPE & TRAITS: _____

STRENGTH: _____

_____

PITFALL: _____

_____

MONEY MINDSET: _____

_____

_____

Note the markings you see in both hands on the blank
hand maps at the back of this book, pages 212–213.

Heart Lines

Magnify Your Relationship Style to Manifest More Money

> *"Money will only make you more of*
> *what you already are."*
> —*T. Harv Eker*

RELATIONSHIPS CONSUME THE majority of our waking lives. Every day we have hundreds of opportunities to connect with other people, including our mates, children, parents, grandparents, siblings, coworkers, bosses, subordinates, business partners and more. Our best relationships start with ourselves.

You can deepen your understanding of your own or someone else's essential relationship or love style by reading one line in the hand—the Heart Line. The simple knowledge you glean from this etching can pick up, perk up and improve your daily interactions. Imagine understanding and embracing your emotional system more intimately and improving your relationships by even ten percent.

Your emotional system began its development in the womb. We now know that embryos are affected by relaxing music, car horns, laughing or shouting family members, and any number of other stimuli. After birth, there are an infinite number of environmental factors that continue to influence emotional growth. Our emotions meander and change from day to day, so think of the Heart Line as a river flowing across a plain. As we mature and change, the shape, length and quality of the Heart Line can and most likely will change as well. You can read your river of the Heart Line to accurately describe your emotional character, tendencies and requirements.

Non-negotiable needs in relationships—such as the need for freedom, connection, consideration or stimulation—are depicted in the Heart Line. It's important you know these needs and that you can claim them for yourself as part of nurturing yourself. If you can clarify and ask for what you need in a relationship, you're more likely to have that need met. And when you care for yourself and your needs are met, you can connect with others more deeply and completely, and therefore appreciate others in a more genuine and compassionate way.

This chapter introduces you to four basic, easy-to-read Heart Line types: the Passionate (Spirited), Big Heart (Nurturer), Hermit (Independent), and Rational Romantic (Thinker). Each represents a style of emotional behavior that is typically displayed to others. How you like to be treated in relationship and how you like to treat others can be read in this line.

Be curious and open to understanding this information, and practice becoming aware of your needs and articulating them in relationships. Be sensitive to others' needs as well. The motivations for connection are different in different people.

I have seen many people who courageously claim their true heart language and live it. It does take bravery to be who you are meant to be. It's not easy, but I'm here to say that living authentically leads to your best life with the most unpretentious relationships at home and in business.

Heart Line Identification

The Heart Line starts on the outer edge of the palm, under the pinkie finger, and runs horizontally across the hand (Figure 95). The line may be long or short, straight or curved. It usually ends somewhere beneath the middle or index finger. Any Heart Line style is possible on a hand. You may also find a different Heart Line on each hand. The type of Heart Line is independent of culture, gender or sexual preference. That means any type of Heart Line can show up on any person from any country, man or woman, gay or straight etc.

The shape of the Heart Line indicates particular emotional styles when relating to others. Curvy lines belong to expressive people who typically show their feelings easily. The Big Heart and Passionate types have curvy lines. They exhibit their feelings more than those with flat

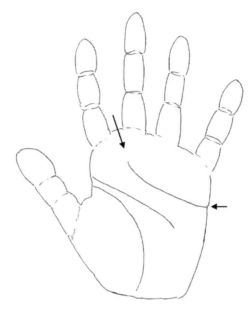

FIGURE 95: THE HEART LINE

or straight Heart Lines. Straight lines belong to people who are more reserved. They display their feelings reluctantly. The Independent and Rational Romantic types have flat Heart Lines. They are less likely to reveal their emotions outwardly.

The description of your style in relationships is determined by the termination point(s) of your Heart Line. Since 2003, I've used the method of placing an imaginary cross on the palm to precisely establish where the Heart Line ends (Figure 96). Find where the widest part of the line ends. Sometimes the line will thin out near the end. To be most precise with your reading, locate the quadrant where the *thickest* part of the Heart Line ends. You'll sometimes see a Heart Line fork into two lines, or even change course; we'll learn more on these formations later in this chapter.

You will want to employ this method on both your right and left hands. Empirical evidence shows that the Heart Line on the right hand demonstrates the emotional characteristics displayed to the world, whereas the left hand most often shows the traits used at home and in the inner, more intimate world.

The imaginary cross creates four quadrants (Figure 96). To position the cross, draw an imaginary line straight down, between the index

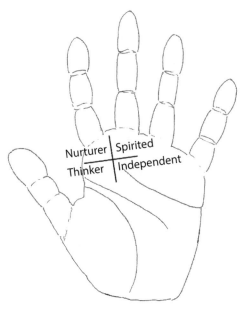

FIGURE 96: NAMES ASSOCIATE WITH THE
TERMINATION POINTS OF THE HEART LINE

and middle fingers, aimed at the bottom center of the palm. Decide whether the Heart Line ends on the index or the middle finger side of the vertical line. Next draw an imaginary horizontal line across the vertical line about half an inch down from base of the fingers. Now determine whether the Heart Line ends above or below the horizontal line.

Using this method, look to see where the Heart Line terminates on each hand. The Heart Line type is named according to where the line ends. These line types correspond to the elements of nature—Earth, Water, Air, and Fire. The names illustrate emotional behaviors found in owners of these lines. As an example, the Heart Line in Figure 96 (above) is short, flat, and ends below the middle finger in the lower right quadrant of the imaginary cross. This is called the Independent Heart.

The Passionate Heart —Spirited

The Passionate Heart Line, associated with the element fire, curves up toward the middle finger (Figure 97). It touches the top of the palm and ends in the upper right quadrant of the imaginary cross, under the middle finger (Figure 96).

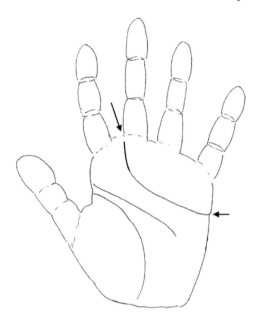

FIGURE 97: PASSIONATE HEART—SPIRITED

If you are the Passionate Heart, you are likely excitable, enthusiastic, expressive and even flirtatious. You have the charisma to be the life of the party. Your natural design is like a campfire, attracting people to your warmth. It's crucial for you to express your wants, even when others don't appreciate your directness. You tend to be happiest when you do expose your desires. Your biggest challenge is being stuck with people you consider boring. You can be so intense that when you feel something passionately, it shows loudly and clearly. A word of caution: that little campfire can turn into a forest fire if not contained or given an appropriate outlet. I remind the Passionate Heart to display his or her wildest passions *and* be considerate of the needs of others.

Prosperity and fulfillment happen in any work position, for the Passionate—Spirited type, if he or she is able to freely express, similar to the flames in a fire. Potential career positions listed with the Fire hand shape would also apply to this fiery Heart Line: artist/creator, marketing consultant, comedian, camp director, party planner, disk jockey, concierge, chef, sports coach, bartender, hair stylist.

STRENGTH: I bring creativity, enthusiasm and spirit to the scene.

PITFALL: Volatility, impulsiveness, unaware of others' emotional needs.

MONEY MINDSET: With free reign I create and inspire exceedingly rich results.

BREAKTHROUGH QUESTIONS: If my fire is feeling put out, how might I redirect my expressive spirit so that I can have more fun and generate greater revenue? Is my dramatic flair feeling over- or under-utilized? If so, what action or thought will bring more balance into my life? How can persistence and consistency help me follow through on my plans to completion?

AFFIRMATION: "Action is the real measure of intelligence." —Napoleon Hill

The Big Heart —Nurturer

The Big Heart (Figure 98), coupled to the element water, curves up toward the index finger. It touches the top of the palm and ends in the

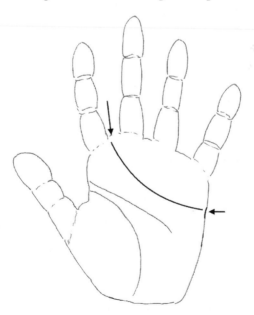

FIGURE 98: BIG HEART—NURTURER

upper left quadrant of the imaginary cross, under the index finger or closer to the index finger than the middle finger (Figure 96).

If you are a Big Heart, you feel emotions keenly and are warm-hearted, caring and nurturing of others. You like connecting with other people and animals. Your favorite song might be "All You Need Is Love" by the Beatles. Your natural design is like a water droplet that joins the pool at the base of a waterfall. Seeing others bond during a special gathering warms your heart. Your feelings are hurt if people sudden-ly disconnect with you or if you witness detachment and conflict be-tween loved ones. Your biggest challenge is to nurture yourself along with others and not fall victim to emotional sell-out. If, in your view, someone disconnects from you abruptly, you might take it personally and become overly critical of yourself, blaming yourself (or the other) for the separation. I remind the Big Heart—Nurturer to look at the truth of the separation or change in the relationship to help him accept himself and all his feelings in all stages of the relationship.

Prosperity and fulfillment happen in any position for the Big Heart—Nurturer type if he or she is able to connect and bond, similar to droplets falling into a pool of water. Potential career positions listed with the Water hand shape would also apply to this Water Heart Line: poet, musician, actor, psychic, photographer, therapist, ballet dancer, life coach, concierge.

STRENGTH: I help people feel loved and cared for, while spending some time alone nurturing myself.

PITFALL: Lost in drama of others, feeling like a victim.

MONEY MINDSET: With heart, I stand firm with my boundaries, collaborating for plenitude.

BREAKTHROUGH QUESTIONS: In any area of my life, am I (with good intention) forcing an emotional connection or response that isn't working? If so, what might I do differently? How would giving others the dignity of their own life curriculum serve me and others? What is my favorite and most rewarding way to help and connect with others?

AFFIRMATION: "It is literally true that you can
succeed best and quickest by helping others succeed." —Napoleon Hill

The Hermit Heart —Independent

The short and straight Heart Line belongs to the Hermit (Figure 99) and is associated with the element earth. It ends below the middle finger, in the lower right quadrant formed by the imaginary cross (Figure 96). The line can end on the horizontal line or slightly above the line to still qualify as the Hermit—Independent.

Women are oftentimes put off by the phrase Hermit because it sounds like they'll be alone their whole lives. If you have a Hermit Heart Line, you are a lone settler. This doesn't mean you will always be alone or that you want to go through life solo. It does mean that you

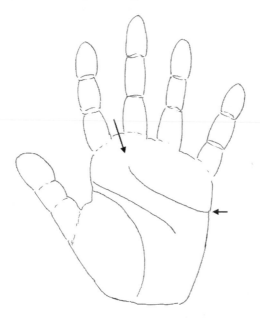

FIGURE 99: HERMIT—INDEPENDENT

prefer working alone and governing your own schedule. The Hermit—Independent certainly has emotions, but you display yours less than do owners of curved Heart Lines. You need time to marinate in your feelings before responding to emotional stimulation. You build loyal, solid and dependable relationships in which you have a strong sense of freedom. In fact, freedom is non-negotiable to you. Your nature is to be productive and grounded. Privacy, security and work are high priorities. You show your love by doing things for others. You assure protection for those few you are loyal to. You might not ask others "How are you feeling?" because you believe that actions speak louder than words. You simply look at how people are doing, without becoming entangled in uncomfortable emotional scenarios. Your biggest challenge is to tune in to your heart and communicate your feelings at the appropriate time of your own volition.

Prosperity and fulfillment happen in any position for the Hermit—Independent type, provided he or she is able to produce in a steady environment, similar to crops growing from the ground. Potential career positions listed with the Earth hand shape would also apply to this Earth Heart Line: laborer, landscaper, construction worker, mason, massage therapist, caregiver, project manager.

> STRENGTH: I am dedicated to projects and my loyalty is rock-solid.
>
> PITFALL: Complete withdrawal when faced with uncomfortable displays of emotion.
>
> MONEY MINDSET: Productivity pays.
>
> BREAKTHROUGH QUESTIONS: I feel most productive when doing these activities… [Make a list.] How could opening my heart a bit more advance my communication skills in a work relationship? How could revisiting a tough emotional conversation with this one person [name] usher in success, security and fortune for me and the team?
>
> AFFIRMATION: "Some people dream of success, while others wake up and work hard at it." —Napoleon Hill

The Rational Romantic—Thinker

The Rational Romantic Heart Line (Fig. 100), linked to the element air, is long, flat and straight, and ends in the lower left quadrant formed by an imaginary cross below the index finger (Figure 96).

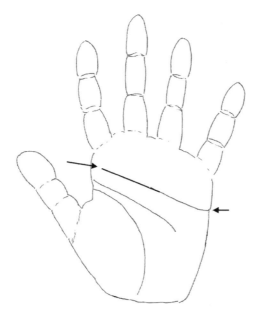

FIGURE 100: RATIONAL ROMANTIC—THINKER

If you own this Heart Line, you are constantly assessing, analyzing, and pondering your own feelings and those of others. You loathe fights because disagreements give you even more to think, think, think about. Your thoughts swirl around you like the wind. Meaningful conversations in which you have time to actually dialog with another person are of utmost importance. Subtle nuances of words or facial expressions can put you into a tailspin of "What did she mean by that?" Your biggest challenge is to minimize your own mental editing. Overly processing feelings comes naturally to the Rational Romantic, and your best trait is consideration. It's very important for you to recognize and respect your own needs and desires and to make requests for those needs to be fulfilled.

Prosperity and fulfillment happen in any position for the Rational Romantic—Thinker type if he or she is able to contribute ideas, comparable to wireless data flowing between sender and receiver. Potential

career positions listed with the Air hand shape would also apply to this
Air Heart Line: principal, teacher, researcher, copywriter, journalist,
orator, writer, analyst, investigator.

> STRENGTH: I am highly considerate, patient and under-
> standing of the thoughts and feelings of others.

> PITFALL: Over-thinking, analysis-paralysis, indecision,
> putting others' needs first 100% of the time.

> MONEY MINDSET: As my thoughts are balanced and
> focused on my projects and planned breakthroughs,
> money blows my way.

> BREAKTHROUGH QUESTIONS: In what ways does my
> consideration for others constructively benefit my career
> or business? Conversely, in what ways does my excessive
> thinking about what everyone else wants hurt my busi-
> ness or career? How can clarification of my needs, while
> also considering others, serve the team *and* me?

> AFFIRMATION: "Unless someone like me cares a whole
> awful lot, nothing is going to get better. It's not."
> —Dr. Seuss

Heart Line Variations

It is not uncommon to see a river veer off in another direction. People
can be like that too. I consider an impersonator to be someone who
subconsciously pretends to be someone he or she is not. Unfortunate-
ly, such a person can develop a deep, long-term pattern of revealing
herself emotionally in ways other than that of her true type as shown
in her Heart Line. It's not who she really is, and this, too, shows up in
the palms.

Spirited Masquerading as Nurturer

A common impersonator is pictured in Figure 101. The curvature of
this Heart Line would seem to end under the dotted arrow. However,
at the last minute the true Heart Line takes a sharp detour toward

the index finger (under the solid arrow), signaling a Passionate Heart masquerading as a Big Heart.

Owners of Heart Lines that change course like this have easy access to two different Heart Line styles—think of a large tributary meeting the main river. Something within them flows in different directions. This Heart Line type is Spirited masquerading as a Nurturer. This person is built to be spontaneous, ask directly for what she wants, and

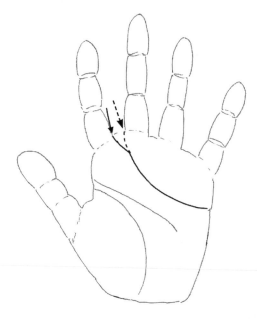

FIGURE 101: SPIRITED IMPERSONATING A NURTURER

display her vivaciousness without hesitation. However, as indicated by the divergent line on her palm, her strong nurturing tendencies typically dominate her emotional style, in which she is concerned about appearing selfish at the expense of others' feelings and desires. She might act to avoid the appearance of being manipulative to get her needs met. Her internal system is a bit confused as to which emotional style to claim.

The upside is that she can play both Spirited and Nurturer. The downside is that she won't feel authentic if she's not in an environment where her impulsive, creative and inspirational self can thrive.

STRENGTH: I fully claim my natural style of spirited expression and release self-imposed obligation to meet the perceived needs of others.

PITFALL: Lost and annoyed wearing the sweetheart mask.

MONEY MINDSET: With grace and ease I skillfully dance between darling and daring to achieve financial objectives.

BREAKTHROUGH QUESTIONS: If impressing others were no longer important to me, what one financial decision would I make, now? What is the simplest, most practical *and* fun way I could create a year's income in the next ninety days? After considering how and with whom I spend my time, would I change anything? If so, what and when?

AFFIRMATION: "When I'm good I'm very, very good, but when I'm bad, I'm better." —Mae West

Chameleon

Another possible Heart Line river system is one that splits into two or three forks. If all parts of the line still have the original width after the split, the owner will easily adapt to the Heart Line styles associated with each termination point.

In Figure 101 the main Heart Line splits under the middle finger into two forks. One fork curves up to the index finger, while the other runs straight, also ending under the index finger. In this case three different Heart Line descriptions apply: Independent, where the split occurs, Nurturer *and* Thinker.

I call this configuration the Chameleon Heart Line. If you see this configuration in your palm, you likely are considerate and cautious in your connections with others. As long as your non-negotiable need for freedom is recognized and protected, you will be balanced in thought, concern and reflection in relationships, and you can adapt as required to the love style around you. If privacy, loyalty, and dependability are needed, you'll naturally find your independent form. If a meaningful conversation is called for, you're all ears. You also have an innate knowl-

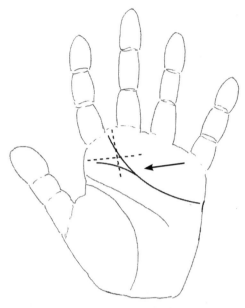

FIGURE 102: CHAMELEON

edge of when a hug would be the perfect medicine. Because you can give up your private sanctuary as you over-adapt to the affectionate needs of others, your internal push–pull requires balancing between your need for independence and social time. I don't know who said this, but it's appropriate here: "Don't change for anyone. Except you. You can change for yourself all you like."

> STRENGTH: Like a chameleon I naturally blend in to any situation, harmonious or adverse, without losing who I am.

> PITFALL: Independence-giveaway, over-adaptive to the needs of others.

> MONEY MINDSET: I impact others in positive and amazing ways; I see great possibilities as I focus my energy toward monetizing ideas and projects.

> BREAKTHROUGH QUESTIONS: If money were sacred to me, how would I treat and value it? What is the most exciting thing about money? How can I champion more

people while focusing my energy toward monetizing ideas and projects?

AFFIRMATION: "Intelligence is the ability to adapt to change." —Stephen Hawking

Betrayal

A strong sense of betrayal resides in the owner of a Heart Line with X's hanging at the start of the Heart Line. The X's can appear on any type of Heart Line.

This pattern indicates problems in the past (or present) with a trusted source—usually a mate or parent. We all understand the sense of being let down by expecting someone to do, say or be something for us, yet they weren't. This marking indicates a deeply disturbing repeating pattern of betrayal where an important person in one's life defied the owner's trust—or perhaps better said, *lied*. An example pattern is a father abandoning a child at eight years old for another family, then in high school the best friend revealed a pinkie-swear-secret leaving the owner with devastating embarrassment. Later in life, after monogamous

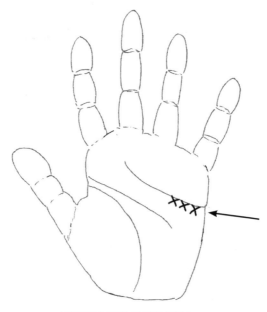

FIGURE 103: BETRAYAL

marriage vows, the owner's mate has a long-lasting affair with either another person or an addictive substance. One of my eighteen-year-old clients with this marking told me that as a highly impressionable and slightly depressive twelve-year-old girl, her older sister declared, "Mom isn't ever coming home," while the mother was on a short business trip. The mother returned, but my client was acutely affected.

The negative possibility is the owner can't shake the likelihood of further betrayal in the present or future. Psychologically, protection mechanisms are constructed to keep others at a distance. In the positive, this sense of betrayal points the owner to be faithful to herself. This sign in the hand is an opportunity to learn to support herself regardless of having an outside system or not. A line in *A Course in Miracles* says, "Love holds no grievances, I will not betray myself."

If you have this marking in your hand, ask yourself, "Is forgiveness a possibility?" Was the person in question doing the best he or she could do under the conditional circumstances? Can you forgive yourself for identifying with the need for someone else to fulfill you? These are deep questions that I have sorted through myself. You are brave to inquire.

I don't remember where I heard this, but I took note. "Forgiveness doesn't mean we condone cruel behavior. However, we may replace the idea of condoning one's behavior with understanding one's behavior." It's okay to despise someone's behavior, but understanding that it happened, even if you don't know why, can release the heavy burden of deep disappointment.

STRENGTH: Awareness of the source of grief and turn around for 100% faith in myself, powerfully supporting myself, no matter what.

PITFALL: Unconscious or conscious prolonged anger and resentment.

MONEY MINDSET: With a free heart, windfalls of money come my way.

BREAKTHROUGH QUESTIONS: When was the first time I sensed betrayal? If I could stand in that person's shoes and imagine the story he or she was telling him or herself at the time, what would it be? Where did he or she

learn to do or say what was done or said? Whose permission do I need to imagine the positive monetary possibilities with a heart fully free from the past? What have
I done with my life that I am really proud of?

AFFIRMATION: I release the past. The past is gone. I trust
myself. I am whole and complete.

You can read about a few other Heart Line configurations in *Your Life
Is In Your Hands: Practical Palm Reading for Purposeful Living*.

Heart Line in Relationships

Now that you've learned your love style, you can better navigate your
own river of connection in relationships with business partners, bosses,
coworkers and clients. Just knowing that everyone has his or her own
relationship style helps because you can see how and why others behave
in certain ways. Being aware of the characteristics of all four Heart Line
quadrants helps you more effectively relate to the people in your life.
I've seen relationships go haywire when one person doesn't realize or
acknowledge that another person has a different style of caring.

If you have felt this way, it might be that you've paired up with your
opposite type, as it is natural to attract, align with and abide in the heart
of our opposites. To determine the opposites, look diagonally to the
sections that are across from each other. Nurturer and Independent are
opposites, and Thinker and Spirited are opposites.

Notice how the emotional style and traits of each Heart Line type
can attract or repel other Heart Line types. It's not uncommon to look
to someone else to express a trait that you feel is lacking in yourself. The
positive behavior of your opposite type will most likely be attractive to
you at first. Over time, however, the very qualities you initially adored
can become irritating because they don't resonate with your own natural style of being, so it's natural to reject them. Perhaps self-criticizing
thoughts exclaim, "I should be more like *that*." That kind of thinking
adds fuel to the inferno of irritation. The remedy is to let go of judgments and accept emotional behaviors that are unlike yours.

In this way, your opposite type opens you up to an expanded ver-
sion of yourself. For example, the Independent is comfortable spending

	Passionate— Spirited		Big Heart— Nurturer	
	Likes	**Dislikes**	**Likes**	**Dislikes**
	Variety	Routine	Bonding	Disconnect
	Banter	Restriction	Closeness	Curtness
	Spontaneity	Wet blankets	Sharing	Withdrawal

	Hermit— Independent		Rational Romantic— Thinker	
	Likes	**Dislikes**	**Likes**	**Dislikes**
	Space	Clinginess	Consistency	Disagreement
	Freedom	Demands	Consideration	Flippancy
	Projects	Fickleness	Conversation	Drama

time alone working on projects. The advanced Independent has learned to keep her heart open, be drawn to the Nurturer (her opposite type), and connect with her partner through heartfelt communication, although she might initiate such communication less frequently than the Nurturer. Conversely, for the Big-Hearted Nurturer it's important to care and cherish, as she loves to do, while also remaining attuned to her center, like the Independent. However, the Nurturer will appear clingy to the Independent, and the Independent will appear heartless to the Nurturer. *Appearance* is the key word and does not indicate truth. The Passionate—Spirited opens up to her opposite by being her naturally dynamic self and making her wants known, while also considering the needs of her partner—a little bit. The Thinker will advance as she considers the needs and emotions of another while also identifying, clarifying and accepting her own desires, like the Passionate. However, there will be many times when the Passionate appears flippant to the Thinker, and the Thinker will appear overly detail oriented to the Passionate.

Of course, you're more than your Heart Line type. But you can see how these emotional differences can interfere with expectations in relationship at home and work. Being true to your emotional style is pivotal in your money-making action steps.

A word of encouragement from Francis of Assisi: "He who works with his hands is a laborer. He who works with his hands and his head is a craftsman. He who works with his hands and his head and his heart is an artist."

Complications will arise if you are not true to your Heart Line type. Consider the ramifications of changing the flow of a river. What would it take for the Colorado or the Mississippi River to change course? It would require colossal landscape changes. Likewise, if you begin acting like a different Heart Line type, trouble will certainly ensue. When starting a relationship, you can suffer from heart-language amnesia. This means you can conform to some ideal you think the other person would like to see in you and forget your true heart language. This state of amnesia is dangerous because it's short lived and the real emotional style will eventually come forward. It's essential, therefore, to live in the real emotional style from day one with any prospective partner.

See how understanding your natural emotional flow and purposely aligning with it can help you improve your relationships. Consider how embracing and integrating the characteristics of your opposite, just a little bit, might help you advance on your love path. Now ponder how your acceptance of others' emotional styles will benefit both you and them. Consider how another person's emotional style is simply his or her way of being. At the beginning of this discussion I asked you to imagine improving your relationships by ten percent. With this new awareness of your own and of opposing emotional styles, you can increase that percentage even further and master your relationships—starting today. Imagine how your mate might respond!

My Money Map Exercise

Using the words in the book, describe some of the key traits, strengths and pitfalls of your Heart Lines. (See the example on page 60.)

The Heart Lines I See in My Hands

Right Hand

PAGE: _____ TRAITS: _____

STRENGTH: _____

_____

PITFALL: _____

_____

MONEY MINDSET: _____

_____

_____

Left Hand

PAGE: _____ TRAITS: _____

STRENGTH: _____

_____

PITFALL: _____

_____

MONEY MINDSET: _____

_____

_____

Note the markings you see in both hands on the blank hand maps at the back of this book, pages 212–213.

Conclusion

Your Life and Your Money Are in Your Hands

> *"Wherever you are, there is everything."*
> —*Sri Nisargadatta Maharaj*

IN CLOSING, the formations in your hands reflect a probable path you will travel with certain behaviors. Understanding the natural and specific-to-you map encoded in your hands will expedite realization of your mental and emotional systems so that you can consciously choose how and when to change course.

When your thoughts about money, or anything you deem important, change, then your storyline, actions and outcomes change. If you think "only the rich get richer," then that is your reality. If you imagine yourself having greater opportunities for fortune and wealth, then that is your reality. While you see yourself as prosperous, you are prosperous. "Whatever man feels deeply or images clearly, is impressed upon the subconscious mind, and carried out in minutest detail," said Florence Scovel Shinn. Present versus future tense thinking is the trick. Watch where you place your attention, like a shepherd's dog watching sheep. Guard and herd as needed to make your dreams a reality.

At the beginning of the book you were given an exercise to write a letter to money starting with "Dear Money." Take a moment to look for correlations between what you learned about your hands and your beliefs.

The unconscious mind stores an enormous reservoir of memories, emotions, thoughts and habits. The key to success is to *use* this book to bridge the hidden and unhidden operations of your mind with the unique map in your hands. Evaluate for yourself. Don't just believe what you are told. Test and prove to yourself. Practically apply what you learned in *Money in Your Hands*. To know what works, track your findings by completing the exercises—more than once.

Use your hands as a reliable roadmap, pointing to a highly plausible parade of natural attitudes and desires, to take conscious charge of your life. If you don't reflect upon and optimize your money-making mindsets and strategies, who will? Your life and your money are truly in your hands.

Appendix

My Hand Map

*Use the blank hand maps on this page and the next page to record the
names and symbols of the markings you see in your hands as you learn
about them in the book. For quick reference, you may want to include
additional information on your hand map such as the page number
and key words. For printable copies of blank hand maps, visit
MoneyInYourHandsBook.com*

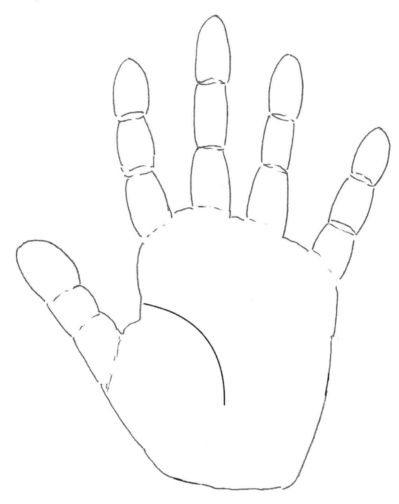

LEFT HAND

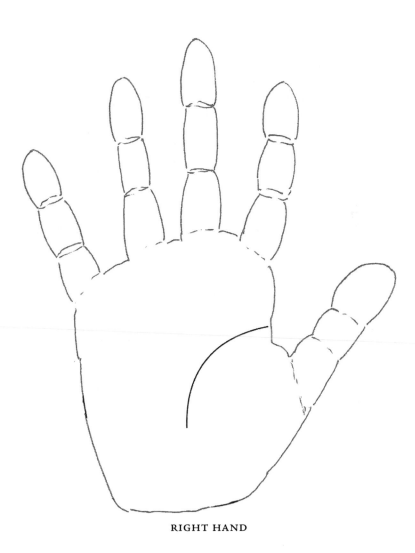

RIGHT HAND

Exercises to Manifest My Money Map and Plan for Financial Freedom

Now is the time to create a strategic plan to generate windfalls of money in very little time. Completing these exercises will make this book work for you! They are intended to help you activate your inner wisdom for financial freedom. Completing some or all of these exercises will help you blend together the interpretations of the markings you identified in your hands. After you understand and accept natural aspects of yourself, you can live your life with less effort and more meaning while creating more wealth.

To complete these exercises most effectively, you may want to set aside some time to dig into them. But if you're short on time, you can simply jot down quick notes and look for threads pointing to an empowering money theme for you. As you fill in the exercises, I encourage you to use the exact words, verbatim, of the descriptions of each marking given in this book. But there is no wrong way to do it. The exercises are designed to guide you step by step to your authentic interior self.

Following are instructions and samples of filled-in exercise sheets. Selecting and blending only three markings is a good way to get started.

For printable copies of blank forms, visit
MoneyInYourHandsBook.com

Sample Exercise 1:
My Money Map Blending Guide
with Strengths and Money Mindsets

To blend three of the most prominent markings you see in your hands refer to the fill-in charts at the end of each chapter, or your journal or notes. After you complete the exercise with three, you may want to add one or two more. Of course, if you're a real go-getter, do this exercise for all of the markings you identified in your hands. You may choose different markings six months from now. For now, allow yourself to start with three. See the example below before you create your own.

I. NAME OF MARKING #I I SEE IN MY HANDS: Intuitively Guided

DESCRIPTION OF MARKING #I: Spiritually motivated

STRENGTH: My intuition is sharp and accurate. I never argue with a hunch.

MONEY MINDSET: I am in the right place at the right time to give and receive prosperity.

2. NAME OF MARKING #2 I SEE IN MY HANDS: Air hand shape

DESCRIPTION OF MARKING #2: Logical, analytical, curious, quick-witted, investigative

STRENGTH: I have an agile mind with the ability to examine, see and comprehend from different perspectives.

MONEY MINDSET: My active mind, clarity in thought, and intellect are highly valued and given due compensation.

BLEND DESCRIPTIONS OF MARKINGS #I AND #2: Intuitively guided, quick-witted, curious, investigative

BLEND STRENGTHS OF MARKINGS #I AND #2: My intuition is sharp and accurate. I never argue with a hunch. I have an agile mind with the ability to examine, see and comprehend from different perspectives.

3. NAME OF MARKING #3 I SEE IN MY HANDS: Long, clear Head
Line, Octopus Brain

DESCRIPTION OF MARKING #3: Multifaceted system of
comprehension and analysis

STRENGTH: I use my exceptional mental aptitude to fully
engage in colossal complexity, successfully synthesizing
large amounts of information.

MONEY MINDSET: I am lavishly compensated as I exercise
my ability to engage in the complex synthesis of
information for the company or my own business.

BLEND MARKINGS #1, #2 AND #3: Intuitively Guided,
considerate (Air hand shape) master problem-solver
(Octopus Brain)

BLEND STRENGTHS OF MARKINGS #1, #2 AND #3: My intuition
is sharp and accurate. I never argue with a hunch. I
have an agile mind with the ability to examine, see
and comprehend from different perspectives. I use my
exceptional mental aptitude to fully engage in colossal
complexity, successfully synthesizing large amounts of
information.

4. MY FAVORITE POTENTIAL POSITIONS FOR EACH MARKING:
Psychologist (Intuitively Guided), investigator (Air hand
shape) criminologist (Octopus Brain)

*If potential positions are not listed for a marking selected, ask yourself to
let an example position come to your mind based on what you learned
about the particular marking in your hands.*

Sample Exercise 2:
My Answers to the Breakthrough Questions

This space is to reflect on breakthrough questions and your answers written with some of the markings you identified in your hands at the end of each chapter. For now, you may wish to identify two or three questions and answers that were most gripping for you.

MARKING: Intuitively Guided

BREAKTHROUGH QUESTION: How might my bank account increase if I align with your intuitive self 10% more often? 50% more often?

MY ANSWER: I'll practice trusting my intuitive self 10% more by setting aside quiet time each morning to tune inward for guidance. I'll make note of new thoughts to help me reach my money goals.

MARKING: Octopus Brain

BREAKTHROUGH QUESTION: When was a time that I felt most fulfilled managing large, important projects with massive amounts of data?

MY ANSWER: When I was writing a How-to book, teaching a certification program including contents of the book and being enrolled in a certification program to investigate and learn more about a particular topic in the book.

Sample Exercise 3:
My Potential Pitfalls

This is a space to identify three (or more) pitfalls you resonated with the most so that you become more conscious of them. Now is the time to take new powerful steps to keep these pitfalls from holding you back. Example: I do have a tendency to spend a lot of time over analyzing and forget to let my inner guidance system show me the way. The pitfall with Intuitively Guided is relying too much on facts and reason. After you name a pitfall identify a course of action to overcome the obstacle with a new mindset, support from a person or realization how a specific instance with the pitfall turned into a tremendous learning experience. For example, with the above example of relying too much on facts and reason, I choose to appreciate my keen abilities to tune inward for inner instruction and will allow time each day to capture hunches I get regarding my business.

MARKING: <u>Intuitively Guided</u>

PITFALL: <u>I do have a tendency to spend a lot of time over analyzing and forget to let my inner guidance system show me the way.</u>

ACTION STEP TO CONQUER THIS PITFALL: <u>I choose to appreciate my keen abilities to tune inward for inner instruction and will allow time each day to capture hunches I get regarding my business.</u>

Sample Exercise 4:
My Action Steps and By When Dates

Identify personal action steps based on your discoveries here. Write down simple steps you'd like to take to improve in any area of your life, be it emotionally, mentally, physically or spiritually in relationships, career, family or anything you think is important. You are encouraged to extend the strengths that you have become more aware of as you filled in the exercises to make them work for you. For example, you may have become clearer about how your natural thinking system (e.g., Octopus Brain) can interact more effectively after realizing that unused octopus limbs tend to create problems to solve in relationships. In this case your action step may be to simply notice when you stir up trouble with a workmate or intimate partner simply to create a problem to solve. Instead, dig into a big complicated problem that you've put off. In this case, don't worry about when you'll take action, just jot down the things you'd like to do as a result of your new awareness.

ACTION STEP: Notice and track how and when I stir up trouble with Sue at work (am I underutilizing my Octopus Brain?)

BY WHEN DATE: End of this week

Exercise 1:
My Money Map Blending Guide
with Strengths and Money Mindsets

Now, reference back to notes you made in the exercises, your hand maps, in a journal, or on your computer. What did you see in your hands?

I. NAME OF MARKING #I I SEE IN MY HANDS: _____

DESCRIPTION OF MARKING #I: _____

STRENGTH: _____

_____

MONEY MINDSET: _____

_____

2. NAME OF MARKING #2 I SEE IN MY HANDS: _____

DESCRIPTION OF MARKING #2: _____

_____

STRENGTH: _____

_____

MONEY MINDSET: _____

_____

BLEND DESCRIPTIONS OF MARKINGS #I AND #2: _____

_____

_____

BLEND STRENGTHS OF MARKINGS #I AND #2: _____

_____

_____

_____

_____

3. NAME OF MARKING #3 I SEE IN MY HANDS: _____

_____

DESCRIPTION OF MARKING #3: _____

_____

STRENGTH: _____

_____

_____

MONEY MINDSET: _____

_____

_____

BLEND MARKINGS #1, #2 AND #3: _____

_____

_____

BLEND STRENGTHS OF MARKINGS #1, #2 AND #3: _____

_____

_____

_____

_____

_____

_____

4. MY FAVORITE POTENTIAL POSITIONS FOR EACH MARKING:

_____

_____

_____

_____

Exercise 2:
My Answers to the Breakthrough Questions

This space is to reflect on a few of the breakthrough questions and your answers written with the markings you identified in your hands at the end of each chapter. For now, you may wish to identify two or three questions that were most gripping for you. Select the questions that will stretch you the most to create the financial independence you want.

MARKING: _____

BREAKTHROUGH QUESTION: _____

_____

_____

_____

MY ANSWER: _____

_____

_____

_____

MARKING: _____

BREAKTHROUGH QUESTION: _____

_____

_____

_____

MY ANSWER: _____

_____

_____

_____

Exercise 3:
Actions to Overcome My Pitfalls

This is a space to identify any pitfalls you most resonated with so that you become more conscious of how you become sabotaged by them. Now is the time to make new choices and take courageous steps to keep these pitfalls from holding you back. After you name a pitfall, identify a course of action to master the obstacle with a new mindset, support from a person or realization how a specific instance with the pitfall turned into a tremendous learning experience.

PITFALL #1: _____

_____

ACTION STEP TO CONQUER THIS PITFALL: _____

_____

PITFALL #2: _____

_____

ACTION STEP TO CONQUER THIS PITFALL: _____

_____

PITFALL #3: _____

_____

ACTION STEP TO CONQUER THIS PITFALL: _____

_____

PITFALL #4: _____

_____

ACTION STEP TO CONQUER THIS PITFALL: _____

_____

Exercise 4:
My Action Steps and By When Dates

Identify personal action steps based on your discoveries as you completed these exercises. Write down simple steps you will take in the next one to three days to improve in any area of your life that will put you closer to your money goals. Emphasize the strengths that you have become more aware of as you filled in the exercises to make them work for you. Assign a by-when date to hold yourself accountable to having that life you most want to live. Block time on your calendar to perform the action steps along with your targeted completion by-when date. Present your self-assigned action steps to an accountability buddy or your business coach to ensure your probabilities for immediate success.

ACTION STEP: _____

_____

_____

BY WHEN DATE: _____

ACTION STEP: _____

_____

_____

BY WHEN DATE: _____

ACTION STEP: _____

_____

_____

BY WHEN DATE: _____

Comprehensive List of Money Mindset Statements

While each money mindset statement is designed to accompany the associated marking described in the book, referring to this complete list should encourage access to deeper awareness around the wealth you want.

I live with joy, as I am balanced in my responsibilities, commitments, integrity and vocation.

I add tremendous value to the family business, and I am worthy of generous compensation for my dedication, loyalty and ability to adapt to change.

I balance my desire to take new classes with determination to generate revenue through financial intelligence.

I am in the right place at the right time to engage in inspirational and meaningful work both to give and receive prosperity.

I am profitable helping people, groups and organizations navigate change because my finesse, experience and skills are highly valued.

I am eager to dig in, carve my unique path and build a solid wealth-generating foundation.

Carving my path to financial freedom is my choice to make and fulfill.

I weigh advice from worthy sources in my tribe and make courageous money decisions.

As a money machine, I consciously create balance in the massive amount of well-paid work I do, and I schedule well-deserved time to play.

I am effectively aligned with successful outcomes to realize maximum riches.

With single-mindedness, I am unstoppable.

With reclaimed power and confidence I eagerly show the way for the highest good of all concerned—and I am financially triumphant.

I am committed to allowing my authentic and inventive self to shine in all areas of my life including wildly successful money-making endeavors.

I balance my want for relationship and self-worth with choices to create more money.

I keep my cool and get back on track after the interruptions are effectively and swiftly handled by me or someone else.

Each week I identify my #1 top revenue-generating task and I commit fully to seeing it through while relishing my success.

I am conscious of where I put my commitments and I stay on track, achieving outstanding results, receiving enormous financial reward.

I see the good in who I am and eagerly apply myself right where I am. Results in revenue are definite.

I accept and appreciate how I apply myself as I align with each project or job and charge what I'm worth in both.

I use my workhorse capabilities to achieve maximum result and return on investment, while honoring my need to rest—a bit.

While I am passionate about my work, I take good care of myself as well as others. I love money and money loves me.

I stretch myself through uncomfortable change and am open to unlimited possibilities as a dedicated money machine.

My power scepter wields focus and muscle to achieve my financial goals.

I carve out the time I need to align with "yes" movement and focus plans toward my financial goals.

With a solid plan I take baby steps forward into new, unexplored directions, committing to new tasks to create colossal amounts of cash. I don't give up.

I love myself enough to say what I want and consistently fortify contracts with heart.

My intelligence is highly valued for safety and security, and I am handsomely paid. Isn't money wonderful?

Through experimentation and play I find my way to create; my bank account grows by leaps and bounds!

The value and volume of my voice fills my velvet purse with endless supply.

With astounding strength for worthy causes, I make an impact in the world, and I'm richly rewarded.

My lively imagination and deep thoughts about the meaning of life are put to wholesome use in an environment that pays exceptionally well.

My warmth and compassion are well balanced with exceptional business sense for attracting astounding wealth.

I use my laser-sharp mind effectively in self-employment or in an occupation where I am highly appreciated and financially compensated.

For the cause, I use my skills of assertive thinking in tactful, savvy ways; limitless riches stream to me.

I am on the road to riches with highly revered solutions.

I am generously compensated as I exercise my ability to engage in the complex synthesis of information for the company or my own business.

With intense drive I can be counted on to gracefully walk the tightrope, as a treasured asset to any team or organization, or as an entrepreneur.

I am crystal clear and well-intended about my business and money goals.

My planning skills lead to increasing promotions and accumulation of material reward. With doggedness I break my glass money ceiling every year!

I am generously compensated monetarily for implementing successful systems, following rules and abiding by policies, at the corporation or within my own business.

I balance my precious time, exacting energy and an endless supply of money with poise and joy.

Optimistically, I shine in my right light and magnetize a jackpot of money.

As I allow my matchless muse to be revealed I am financially gladdened as a one-of-a-kind creative.

I use my natural communication skills and insights to structure deals and swiftly handle financial complexity.

I settle for nothing less than top dollar for access to my quick, sharp and clever strategizing expertise.

I enjoy the financial rewards of super-achievement with the most fitting people in my empire where everyone thrives.

With grace and ease I stand in the truth of my value and produce generous payouts for everyone, including myself.

I invite and allow windfalls of wealth for the distinctiveness I bring forward, inspiring wholeness in myself and others.

I bring rich compensation to the causes I stand for drawing upon the Warrior within.

As a master messenger to the masses I magnetize money.

My psychological and spiritual insights are highly valuable and I charge what I'm worth (and get it), facilitating astounding results.

I am well rewarded as a gifted seer, sharing my spiritual wisdom in a receiving atmosphere.

I am richly rewarded for my gift of introspection, seeing what needs to be destroyed in order to create room for what needs to be born.

My business of intuiting leads me to a bounty of fortune.

The magic money purse I imagine in my mind manifests triple-fold in my life.

I am lavishly compensated for the accidental discoveries that magically come my way.

I am richly rewarded for my willingness to remain open to deep emotion and my availability to other lost souls ready to "come back to life" again, feeling joy.

I am gifted in ways that facilitate transformation and triumph for both myself and others.

I cleverly negotiate for top dollar for access to my gift of special ingenuity and highly complex code-cracking.

Prosperity surrounds me as I take effective action based on my infinite wisdom.

I stretch into sharing my extraordinary understanding with the right forum and am generously compensated.

I gladly receive payment for my gift of insight, knowing the relief experienced through interaction with my abilities.

I intend. It happens. Bam!

Currency floods to me as my voice carries through the airwaves.

I am paid handsomely for my strong sense of loyalty, protective instincts, commonsense nature, and the strength of my hands.

My active mind, clarity in thought, and intellect are highly valued and given due compensation.

I am appreciated and highly compensated for my eye for detail, compassion, care and sensitivity to the needs of others.

In the right setting, my spirited nature and a sense of joyful accomplishment are applauded with big bucks.

With free reign I create and inspire exceedingly rich results.

With heart, I stand firm with my boundaries, collaborating for plentitude.

Productivity pays.

As my thoughts are balanced and focused on my projects and planned breakthroughs, money blows my way.

With grace and ease I skillfully dance between darling and daring to achieve financial objectives.

I impact others in positive and amazing ways; I see great possibilities as I focus my energy towards monetizing ideas and projects.

With a free heart, windfalls of money come my way.

Resources

Eker, T. Harv, *Secrets of the Millionaire Mind: Mastering the Inner Game of Wealth*. New York, NY, Harper Collins, 2005.

Hill, Napoleon, *Think and Grow Rich*. New York, NY, Ballantine Books, 1993.

Hirsch, Jennifer, *God Given Glyphs*. Johannesburg, South Africa, Muse Press, 2014.

Mahabal, Vernon, *The Secret Code on Your Hands: An Illustrated Guide to Palmistry*. San Rafael, CA, Mandala Publishing, 2007.

Packard, Kay, *Your Life Is In Your Hands: Practical Palm Reading for Purposeful Living*. Three Rivers, CA, Pioneer Press, 2015

Robin, Vicki, and Dominguez, Joe, *Your Money or Your Life: Nine Steps to Transforming Your Relationship with Money and Achieving Financial Independence*. New York, NY, Penguin Books, 2018.

Shinn, Florence Scovel, *Your Word is Your Wand*. Asherville, NC, Center for Spiritual Living, 1928

Shinn, Florence Scovel, *The Game of Life and How to Play It*. Freely distributed through Florenceshinn.com

Sincero, Jen, *You are a Badass at Making Money: Master the Mindset of Wealth*. New York, NY, Penguin Random House, 2017.

Visit MoneyInYourHandsBook.com

About the
American Academy of Hand Analysis

THE AMERICAN ACADEMY of Hand Analysis (AAHA) is dedicated to sharing and teaching the sacred art and science of hand analysis, elevating consciousness through deep personal awareness and purposeful living and helping people become their best selves by seeing who they are from the inside out.

AAHA offers a series of step-by-step learning programs, in person and through online webinars, that teach students to read and interpret the information etched into the hands and fingerprints, enabling practitioners to help people live empowered lives.

AAHA and its training courses are recognized internationally for their leadership in bringing out the best in people by teaching them to become more conscious of who they are. The ultimate goal of AAHA's training programs is self-realization, helping people find answers to essential questions such as: Why am I here? What is my purpose? How can I live into my highest potential?

The paradigm of the American Academy of Hand Analysis is both profound and simple: It starts with you. Come discover, explore, awaken and illuminate your life—on purpose! To learn more about AAHA and its programs, visit www.AcademyofHandAnalysis.org.

Notes